Table of Contents

Autobiography of a Child

Hannah Lynch

Chapter I. LOOKING BACKWARD.

The picture is clear before me of the day I first walked. My mother, a handsome, cold-eyed woman, who did not love me, had driven out from town to nurse's cottage. I shut my eyes, and I am back in the little parlour with its spindle chairs, an old-fashioned piano with green silk front, its pink-flowered wall-paper, and the two wonderful black-and-white dogs on the mantelpiece. There were two pictures I loved to gaze upon—Robert Emmett in the dock, and Mary Stuart saying farewell to France. I do not remember my mother's coming or going. Memory begins to work from the moment nurse put me on a pair of unsteady legs. There were chairs placed for me to clutch, and I was coaxingly bidden to toddle along, "over to mamma." It was very exciting. First one chair had to be reached, then another fallen over, till a third tumbled me at my mother's feet. I burst into a passion of tears, not because of the fall, but from terror at finding myself so near my mother. Nurse gathered me into her arms and began to coo over me, and here the picture fades from my mind.

My nurse loved me devotedly, and of course spoiled me. Most of the villagers helped her in this good work, so that the first seven years of my childhood, in spite of baby-face unblest by mother's kiss, were its happiest period. Women who do not love their children do well to put them out to nurse. The contrast of my life at home and the years spent with these rustic strangers is very shocking. The one petted, cherished, and untroubled; the other full of dark terrors and hate, and a loneliness such as grown humanity cannot understand without experience of that bitterest of all tragedies—unloved and ill-treated childhood. But I was only reminded of my sorrow at nurse's on the rare occasion of my mother's visits, or when nurse once a month put me into my best clothes, after washing my face with blue mottled soap—a thing I detested—and carried me off on the mail-car to town to report my health and growth. This was a terrible hour for me. From a queen I fell to the position of an outcast. My stepfather alone inspired me with confidence. He was a big handsome man with a pleasant voice, and he was always kind to me in a genial, thoughtless way. He would give me presents which my mother would angrily seize from me and give to her other children, not from love, for she was hardly kinder to them than to me, but from an implacable passion to wound, to strike the smile from the little faces around her, to silence a child's laughter with terror of herself. She was a curious woman, my mother. Children seemed to inspire her with a vindictive animosity, with a fury for beating and banging them, against walls, against chairs, upon the ground, in a way that seems miraculous to me now how they were saved from the grave and she from the dock.

She had a troop of pretty engaging children, mostly girls, only one of whom she was ever known to kiss or caress, and to the others she was worse than the traditional stepmother of fairy tale. It was only afterwards I learned that those proud creatures I, in my abject solitude, hated and envied, lived in the same deadly fear of her with which her cold blue eyes and thin cruel lips inspired me with.

But there were, thank God! many bright hours for me, untroubled by her shadow. I was a little sovereign lady in my nurse's kindly village, admired and never thwarted. I toddled imperiously among a small world in corduroy breeches and linsey skirts, roaming unwatched the fields and lanes from daylight until dark. We sat upon green banks and made daisy chains, and dabbled delightedly with the sand of the pond edges, while we gurgled and chattered and screamed at the swans.

The setting of that nursery biography is vague. It seemed to me that the earth was made up of field beyond field, and lanes that ran from this world to the next, with daisies that never could be gathered, they were so many; and an ocean since has impressed me less with the notion of immensity of liquid surface than the modest sheet of water we called the Pond. Years afterwards I walked out from town to that village, and how small the pond was, how short the lanes, what little patches for fields so sparsely sprinkled with daisies! A more miserable disillusionment I have not known.

I have always marvelled at the roll of reminiscences and experiences of childhood told consecutively and with coherence. Children live more in pictures, in broken effects, in unaccountable impulses that lend an unmeasured significance to odd trifles to the exclusion of momentous facts, than in story. This alone prevents the harmonious fluency of biography in an honest account of our childhood. Memory is a random vagabond, and plays queer tricks with proportion. It dwells on pictures of relative unimportance, and revives incidents of no practical value in the shaping of our lives. Its industry is that of the idler's, wasteful, undocumentary, and untrained. For vividness without detail, its effects may be compared with a canvas upon which a hasty dauber paints a background of every obscure tint in an inextricable confusion, and relieves it with sharply defined strokes of bright colour.

Jim Cochrane, my everyday papa, as I called him, was a sallow-faced man with bright black eyes, which he winked at me over the brim of his porter-measure, as he refreshed himself at the kitchen fire after a hard day's work. He was an engine-driver, and once took me on the engine with him to the nearest station, he and a comrade holding me tight between them, while I shrieked and chattered in all the bliss of a first adventure.

This is a memory of sensation, not of sight. I recall the rush through the air, the sting, like needle-points against my cheeks and eyelids, of the bits of coal that flew downward from the roll of smoke, the shouting men laughing and telling me not to be afraid, the red glare of the furnace whenever they slid back the grate opening, the whiff of fright and delight that thrilled me, and, above all, the confidence I had that I was safe with nurse's kind husband.

Poor Jim! His was the second dead face I looked upon without understanding death. The ruthless disease of the Irish peasant was consuming him then, and he died before he had lived half his life through.

Chapter II. MARY JANE.

Mary Jane was my first subject and my dearest friend. She lived in a little cottage at the top of the village that caught a tail-end view of the pond and the green from the back windows.

It is doubtful if I ever knew what calling her father followed, and I have forgotten his name. But Mary Jane I well remember, and the view from those back windows. She was older than I, and was a very wise little woman, without my outbursts of high spirits and inexplicable reveries. She had oiled black curls, the pinkest of cheeks, and black eyes with a direct and resolute look in them, and she read stories that did not amuse or interest me greatly, because they were chiefly concerned with good everyday boys and girls. She tried to still a belief in fairies by transforming them into angels, but she made splendid daisy chains, and she could balance herself like a bird upon the branches that overhung the pond.

Here she would swing up and down in fascinating peril, her black curls now threatening confusion with the upper branches, her feet then skimming the surface of the water. It was a horrible joy to watch her and calculate the moment when the water would close over branch and boots and curls.

My first attempt to imitate her resulted in my own immersion, and a crowd to the rescue from the nearest public-house. After the shock and the pleasant discovery that I was not drowned, and was really nothing the worse for my bath, I think I enjoyed the sensation of being temporarily regarded in the light of a public personage. But Mary Jane howled in a rustic abandonment to grief. She told me afterwards she expected to be taken to prison, and believed the Queen would sentence her to be hanged. It took longer to comfort her than to doctor me.

It was some time after that before I again attempted to swing upon the branches over the pond, but contented myself with feeding the swans from the bank upon a flat nauseous cake indigenous to the spot, I believe, which a shrivelled old woman used to sell us at a stall hard by. There were flower-beds and a rural *châlet* near the pond, which now leads me to conclude that the green was a single-holiday resort, for I remember a good deal of cake-crumbs, orange-peels, and empty ginger-beer bottles about the place.

The old woman was very popular with us. Even when we had no pennies to spend, she would condescend to chat with us as long as we cared to linger about her stall of delights, and she sometimes wound up the conversation by the gift of our favourite luxury, a crab-apple.

I fear there was not one of us that would not cheerfully have signed away our future both here and hereafter for an entire trayful of crab-apples. Each tray held twelve, placed two and two, like school-ranks; and I know not which were the more bewitching to the eye, the little trays or the demure double rows of little apples. The child rich enough to hold out a pinafore for Bessy to wreck this harmony of tray and line by pouring twelve heavenly balls into it, asked nothing more from life in the way of pleasure.

The pride of Mary Jane's household was an album containing views of New York, whither Mary Jane's eldest brother had gone. New York, his mother told us, was in America. The difficulty for my understanding was to explain how any place so big as New York could find another place big enough to stand in. Why was New York in America and not America in New York?

Neither Mary Jane nor her mother could make anything of my question. They said you went across the sea in a ship to New York, and when they added that the sea was all water, I immediately thought that they must mean the pond, and that if I once got to the other side of it I should probably find America and New York.

Until then I had believed the other side of the pond to be heaven, because the sky seemed to touch the tops of the trees. But it was nicer to think of it as America, because there was a greater certainty of being able to get back from America than from heaven,—above all, when I was so unexpectedly made acquainted with the extremely disagreeable method by which little children are transported thither.

I do not know where nurse can have taken Mary Jane and me once. I have for years cherished the idea that it was to Cork, which was a long way off; but I am assured since that she never took me anywhere in a train, and that certainly I never was in Cork.

This is a mystery to me, for the most vivid recollection of those early years is a train journey with nurse and Mary Jane. I remember the train steaming slowly into a station: the hurry, the bustle, the different tone of voices round me, and Mary Jane's knowing exclamation, "Angela, this is Cork, one of the biggest towns of Ireland—as fine, they say, as Dublin."

Now, if I were never in Cork, never travelled with nurse and

Mary Jane, will any one explain to me how I came to remember those words so distinctly? Odder still, I am absolutely convinced that nurse took my hand in an excited grasp, and led me, bewildered and enchanted, through interminable streets full of such a diversity of objects and interests as dazed my imagination like a blow. Not that I was unacquainted with city aspects; but this was all so different, so novel, so much more brilliant than the familiar capital!

I remember the vivid shock of military scarlet in a luminous atmosphere, and smiling foreign faces, and several ladies stopped to look at me and cry, "Oh, the little angel!" I was quite the ideal wax doll, pretty, delicate, and abnormally fair. I believe Mary Jane worshipped me because of the whiteness of my skin and for my golden hair.

Memories of this journey I never made and of this town I never visited do not end here. After eternal wanderings through quite the liveliest streets I have ever known, without remembrance of stopping, of entrance or greetings, I find myself in an unfamiliar room with nurse, Mary Jane, a strange lady, and my mother. My mother was dressed in pale green poplin, and looked miraculously beautiful. I know the dress was poplin, because nurse said so when I touched the long train and wondered at its stiffness.

She looked at me coldly, and said to nurse—

"That child has had sunstroke. I never saw her so red. You must wash her in new milk."

Whereupon she rang a bell, and cried out to somebody I did not see to fetch a basin of milk and a towel. I shuddered at the thought that perhaps my mother would wash my face instead of nurse, for I dreaded nothing so much as contact with that long white hand of sculptural shape.

Among the mysteries of my life nothing seems so strange to me as the depth of this physical antipathy to my mother. The general reader to whom motherhood is so sacred will not like to read of it. But to suppress the most passionate instinct of my nature, would be to suppress the greater part of my mental and physical sufferings. As a baby I went into convulsions, I am told, if placed in my mother's arms. As a child, a girl, nothing has been so dreadful to me as the most momentary endurance of her touch.

Once when I was threatened with congestion of the brain from over-study, I used to lie in frenzied apprehension of the feel of her hand on my brow, and she was hardly visible in the doorway before a nervous shudder shook my frame, and voice was left me to mutter, "Don't touch me! oh, don't touch me!" Her glance was quite as repulsive to me, and I remember how I used to feel as if some one were walking over my grave the instant those unsmiling blue eyes fell upon me. An instinct stronger than will, even in advanced girlhood, inevitably compelled me to change my seat to get without their range.

I recall this feeling, to-day quite dead, as part of my childhood's sufferings, and I wonder that the woman who inspired it should in middle life appear to me a woman of large and liberal and generous character, whose foibles and whose rough temper in perspective have acquired rather a humorous than an antipathetic aspect. But children, but girls, are not humorists, and they take life and their elders with a lamentable gravity.

On this occasion it was my mother who washed my face in new milk. The fragrance and coolness of the milk were delicious, if only a rougher and coarser hand had rubbed my cheeks.

While still submitting to the process, I stared eagerly round the room. There was a grand piano in black polished wood, the sofa was blue velvet and black wood, and the carpet a very deep blue. The air smelt of gillyflowers, and there were big bunches in several vases. Yet my mother assures me she never met me at Cork or elsewhere, never washed my face in new milk, is unacquainted with that black piano, the blue velvet sofa, and the gillyflowers.

She admits she did possess a pale green robe of poplin with an enormous train, bought for a public banquet given to distinguished Americans, but doubts if I ever saw it. Nurse, whom I questioned years after, laughed at the idea as at a nightmare.

Still that journey to Cork, Mary Jane's words and my mother's, the bowl of new milk, the green poplin dress, the blue-and-black sofa, the grand piano, and the gillyflowers, remain the strongest haunting vision of those years.

The first sampler I ever saw was worked by Mary Jane. I associate the alphabet in red and green wool with shining blue-black curls behind a bright-green tracery of foliage upon a blue sky.

Mary Jane used to sit upon a high bank, and work assiduously at her sampler. I thought her achievement very wonderful, but I own I never could see anything in coloured wools and a needle to tempt an imaginative child. So much sitting still was dull, and the slow growth of letters or sheep or flowers exasperating to young nerves on edge. My affection for Mary Jane, however, was so strong, that I gallantly endeavoured to learn from her, but it was in the butterfly season, and there was my friend Johnny Burke racing past after a splendid white butterfly.

What was the letter "B" in alternate stitches of red and green in comparison with the capture of that butterfly?

So the child, the poet tells us, is always mother of the woman, and not even the sane and sobering influence of the years has taught me that serious matters are of greater consequence than the catching of some beautiful butterfly. As I bartered childhood to agreeable impulses, so have I bartered youth and middle age, and if I now am a bankrupt in the face of diminishing impulses, who is to blame, after all, but perverse and precarious nature?

What became of Mary Jane I have never known. Upon my memory she is eternally impaled: a child of indefinite years from eight to eleven, with oily ringlets and clear black eyes, pink-cheeked, smiling, over-staid for her age (except in the matter of swinging recklessly over the pond), working samplers, telling a group of unlettered babies exceedingly moral tales, devoted to me and to a snub-nosed doll I abhorred; with inexhaustible gifts, including a complete knowledge of the views of New York, an enthusiasm for that mysterious being Mary Stuart, and an acquaintance with national grievances vaguely embodied in a terror of Queen Victoria's power over her Irish subjects.

She must have grown into a woman of principle and strong views.

Chapter III. MY BROTHER STEVIE.

I must have been about five when my sovereignty was seriously threatened by the coming of Stevie. The ceremony of arrival I do not remember. He seems to have started into my life like Jack out of his box to kneel for ever in his single attitude,—upon a sofa, with his elbows on a little table drawn up in front of the sofa, and his head resting either on one or both palms.

Do not ask me if he ever slept, lay down, or walked as other children. I have no memory of him except kneeling thus upon the parlour sofa, looking at me or out of the window with beautiful unearthly eyes of the deepest brown, full of passionate pain and revolt. Only for my tender nurse did this fierce expression soften to a wistfulness still more sad.

That Stevie's head was impressive, almost startlingly great, even eyes so young as mine could discern. Auburn hair the colour of rich toned wood, that only reveals the underlying red when the sun or firelight draws it out, and looks like heavy shadow upon a broad white forehead when no gleam is upon it; strong features not pinched but beautified by disease, and a depth and eloquence of regard such as are rarely looked for under children's lids.

The head expressed not pathos so much as tragedy. The frame I never saw; I cannot tell if Stevie were tall or dwarfed. A tipsy town nurse had dropped him down the length of two long flights of stairs, and a strong child's back was broken.

He did not bear his sorrow patiently, I fear, but with sullen courage and with a corrosive silent fretting. He hated me in envy of my health and nimble limbs, but what he hated still more than even the sight of my vivacious pleasures was any question about his health. I never saw a glance so deadly as that with which he responded to the kindly hope of Mary Jane's mamma that his back was feeling better. If a look could kill, Mary Jane had been motherless on the spot.

But alas for me! no longer a sole sovereign. My serene *al fresco* kingdom was invaded by the darker passions. I did not like Stevie. He was a boy a little girl might be sorry for in her better moments, but could not love.

He was querulous whenever I was near, and had a spiteful thirst for whatever I had set my heart upon. Nurse transferred the better part of her affection and attention to him. This was as it should be, but I was sadly sore about it in those unreasoning times.

The little packages of round hard sweets in transparent glazed paper, pink and violet, that Jim Cochrane used to bring me home from the big shop we called the Co. (*i. e.*, Co-operative Store), were now offered to Stevie, who took all my old privileges as his due.

Even Mary Jane would sit on the window-sill, when she should have been playing with me outside, and gaze at him in prolonged owlish fascination, drawn by the fierce pain of those suffering eyes, with their terrible tale of revolt and anger. Stevie got into the way of tolerating Mary Jane's society.

You see she could sit still for hours; she was a quiet little body who enjoyed her sampler and a book—not a creature of nerves, that raced and danced through the hours and was dropped into slumber by exhausted limbs. He would even let Mary Jane sit at his table and stroke his white hand with an air of deprecating tenderness, while he stared silently out upon the noisy green, where boys and girls were romping with straight backs and strong limbs.

What wonder this poor little fellow with the soul of a buccaneer hated us all. Did his favourite books, read and re-read, not amply reveal his tastes, though of these he never spoke? The lust of travel, of adventure, of daring deed filled his dreaming, and yet he never had the courage to ask a soul if he should one day be well and fit to meet the glory of active manhood.

Let remembrance dwell rather with this thought than upon the darker side of his temper, upon the subtle cruelty of the glance that met mine, upon the quiver of baffled desire that shook his fine nostrils and the vindictive clutch of his bloodless fingers whenever I thoughtlessly raced near him. If he gave me my first draught of the soul's bitters, I still owe him pity and sympathy, and I had my pleasures abroad to console me for his hate.

There were the wide fields and the birds, the swans on the pond, our friend the applewoman, and a band of merry shock-headed playmates outside for me. There were the seasons for my choosing: the spring lanes in their bloomy fragrance; the warm summer mornings, when it was good to sit under trees and pretend to be a bewitched palace waiting for the coming of the prince, or dabble on the brim of pool edges; the autumn luxuriance of fallen leaves, which lent the charmed excitement of rustle to our path along the lanes: and the frost of winter, with the undying joys of sliding and snowballs and the fun of deciphering the meaning of Jack Frost's beautiful pictures on the window-panes and his tricks upon the branches.

If Stevie disliked my restlessness, it gave him great satisfaction to despise my artistic sensibilities, and jeer at my lack of learning. I adored music, and often amused myself for hours at a time crooning out what I must have conceived as splendid operas, until my voice would break upon a shower of tears.

I naturally thought my wordless singing must be very beautiful to move me to such an ecstasy of emotion, and I think I enjoyed the tears even more than my melancholy howling. But Stevie did not. On the first occasion of this odd performance, he watched me in a convulsion of unjoyous laughter.

"What an awful fool you are, Angela!" he hissed, when he saw the pathetic tears begin to roll quickly down my cheeks. I rushed from the parlour, and the sweet water of artistic emotion turned into the bitter salt of chagrin.

I must have inherited this tendency from my mother's father, a music-daft Scotsman, who was never quite sure whether he was Hamlet or Bach. At long intervals he would stroll out of town by the Kildare road in an operatic cloak and a wide-leafed sombrero, to inspect us. He had a notion that I, if left to my own devices, might turn out a second Catherine Hayes, and after his visits I invariably returned to my dirges and cantatas with ardour.

During the year that Stevie lived at nurse's, visits from the people I significantly called my Sunday parents (because, I suppose, I wore my Sunday frock and shoes in their honour) were more frequent. Golden-haired little ladies, in silk frocks and poky bonnets, came and looked at me superciliously. The bland hauteur of one of those town creatures in superior raiment once maddened me to that degree (it was the dog-days, no doubt) that I walked up to the chair on which she complacently sat, and hit her cheek.

This naturally afforded my mother an excuse for pronouncing me dangerous and prolonging my absence from the family circle.

I was, I will admit, a desperate little spitfire, full of uncontrollable passion. But I had some rudimentary virtue, I am glad to know. I never lied, and I was surprisingly valiant for a delicately-built little girl.

I cannot remember the period of transition, but I suddenly see Stevie in quite a new part. The vitality and unfathomable yearning burnt themselves out of his eyes, and there was a wearied gentleness in them even for me. He would watch me quiescently without envy or bitterness, and speak to me in slow unfamiliar tones. He turned with indifference from his books, and seemed to know no active desires.

"Does your back hurt, Stevie?" I asked, staring at him solemnly. Even now I can feel the moving sadness of his grave look.

"It always hurts;" and then he added, with a ring of his old spite, "but you needn't be sorry for me, Angela."

"I am sorry, ever so sorry, Stevie," I sobbed, not knowing why.

"I wasn't good to you at all," he muttered, dreamily.

"Oh, I don't mind now. I'm fonder of you, Stevie. I wish you'd get well, I do. I wouldn't mind being ill to keep you company."

"I think I'd be fond of you, Angela, if I got well. Would you mind," he looked at me uneasily for help in his awkwardness, and then a little pink colour came into his cheek, and he spoke so low that it was hard to hear him—"I think I'd like you to put your arms round my neck and kiss me, Angela."

It was our first kiss and our last. The impulsive affection of my embrace pleased him, and he kept my cheek near his for some moments, while in silence we both gazed out upon the blotch of dusty green that mingled with the pale blue of the sky. I feared to move or even wink an eyelid, this new mood of Stevie's so awed me.

"You may have my books and my penknife," said Stevie, breaking the spell. "They're awful nice books. Grandpa gave them to me. I'll explain the pictures to-morrow. But perhaps you wouldn't like boys' books, Angela," he said, dejectedly, and scanned my face in a humble way.

"Oh yes, I would," I cried, eagerly.

"Then you'll be fonder of me," he sighed, satisfied. "Grandpa once read me about a little boy that was ill like me, and he had a sister. He was very fond of her. He didn't hate people that are well, like me, but I don't think that's true, Angela. A boy can't feel good and nice if he is always in pain, can he? It wouldn't be so hard for little girls, for they don't mind sitting still so much."

This, I think, is how he talked, musingly, with none of the old vehement revolt of voice and glance that still lingers with me as the most vivid interpretation of his personality.

"I can't believe any boy was ever like that queer little fellow. I wonder, if grandpa knew I wanted it very much, would he bring out that book and read it all over again to me. I want to see if it's realler."

I drew my arms away from his neck, and ran off screaming for nurse to drive into town, and tell grandpa to come and read about a sick little boy to Stevie.

Nurse came to him, ready to do his slightest behest. I still see her standing looking at him anxiously, and see lifted to her that awful quietude of gaze, out of a face sharply thinned so suddenly.

"Bring me some gingerbread-nuts and lots of pipes to blow bubbles with," he said, and I felt the childish request soothed nurse's alarm.

"Faith, an' ye'll have them galore, my own boy," she cried, "if nurse has to walk barefoot to Dublin for them."

Mary Jane's mother came over to stay with us while nurse drove off to town. Stevie knelt in his eternal position, with his cheek against his open palm and cushions piled around him. He did not speak, but stared out of the window.

I went and sat with "Robinson Crusoe" on the window-ledge, to watch nurse's departure and wave my hand to her. Not to wave my hand from the window and blow kisses to her would be to miss the best part of the fun of this unexpected incident.

The world outside rested in the unbroken stillness of noon. When nurse was out of sight, I turned to acquaint Stevie with the fact. His eyes were shut. So he remains in my memory, a kneeling statue of monumental whiteness and stillness.

A strange way for a little lad to die! Not a sigh, not a stir of hand or body, not a cry, no droop of head or jaw. A long, silent stare upon the sunny land, lids quietly dropped, and then the long unawakeable sleep. To my thinking it was an ideal close to a short life of such unrest and pain and misery. It was indeed rest robbed of all the horrors of death.

The horror remained for one who loved him, and this was no blood relative, but an ignorant nurse. Mary Jane's mamma came to see how matters were with the children. Stevie, as I thought, still slept, kneeling with his cheek upon his palm, and elbow resting on a cushion between it and the table. She looked at him quickly, flung up her hands, and trembled from head to foot. Then she bethought herself of me, and ordered me to go and sit with my book in the garden, and keep very still.

That was a long afternoon. I thought nurse would never come back. I had looked at all the pictures, spoken to each flower, hunted for ladybirds, and solaced myself with operatic diversion. Now I wanted to go back to Stevie, but the door was shut against me and the blinds were all drawn down, though it was not night—the sun had not even begun to dip westward.

Judge my delight to catch the sound of wheels along the road. I raced down to the gate to meet nurse and see all the wonders from town. Grandpa was not with her, and she came up the little path swinging her basket blithely.

"They knew the book at once, and I've got it—'tis by a man called Dickens. Your grandpa and mamma will come to-morrow and read it. They're giving a grand party to-night. Such a power of flowers and jellies and things. But the pipes I've brought Stevie in dozens and gingerbread-nuts galore."

Then her eye fell upon the blinded windows, and the colour flew from her blooming rustic face. She was nearly as white as Stevie inside. She flung away her basket, and the pipes, the book, and cakes rolled out on the gravel, to my amazement. More wonderful still, she broke out in wild guttural sounds and whirled around in a dance of madness.

I had never seen a grown person behave so oddly, and it enchanted me. I caught her skirt and began to spin round too in an ecstasy of shrill sympathy. She looked down at me in a queer wild way, as if she had never seen me before and resented my kindness, and then she cast me from her with such unexpected force that I fell among the flower-beds, too astounded to cry. Decidedly, grown-up people, I reflected, are hard to understand.

I had given up wondering at all the unusual things that happened the rest of that day. People kept coming and going, and spoke softly, often weeping. Nobody paid the least attention to me, though I repeatedly asserted that I was hungry. Then at last a comparative stranger took me into the kitchen, and made me a bowl of bread and milk. She forgot the sugar, and I was very angry. Big people often do forget the essential in a thoughtless way.

Men, too, came pouring in, and talked in undertones,

looking at me as if I had been naughty. I resented those looks quite as much as the unwonted neglect of my small person, and was cheered, just upon the point of tears, by the appearance of Mary Jane, who invited me to go home and sleep with her that night.

I did not object. I never objected to any fresh excitement, and I was fond of Mary Jane's brindled cat. But why did Mary Jane cry over me and treat me as a prisoner all next day? She managed to keep me distracted in spite of her tears, and I slept a second night with the brindled cat in my arms, quite happy.

The second day of imprisonment did not pass so well. I was restless, and wanted to see Stevie again. I wanted several things that nobody seemed to understand, and I moped in a corner and wept, miserable and misunderstood. On the morning of the third day I could bear my lot no longer. I scorned Mary Jane's hollow friendship, and ran away without hat or jacket.

Outside nurse's gate knots of villagers were gathered in their best clothes. It looked like Sunday. I ran past them and shot in through the open hall-door. Nobody saw me, and I made straight for Stevie's room, which he never left before noon. I felt a rogue, and smiled in pleased recognition of the fact. How glad Stevie would be to see me!

The door was ajar, and I entered cautiously. On Stevie's bed I saw a long queer box with a lid laid beside it, and there was quite a quantity of flowers, and tapers were lit upon a table beside the bed. Was Stevie going away? But what use were candles when the sun was shining as brightly as possible?

I wanted to see what was inside the box, and drew over a chair which enabled me to climb upon the bed. Anger shook me like a frenzy. To put sick Stevie in a horrid box! Whoever heard of such a monstrous thing? It was worse than any of the dreadful things the wicked fairies did in stories.

They had taken care, I noted, to pad the box with nice white satin to make it soft; and they put a pretty new nightgown, with satin and white flowers all over it, on Stevie. All the same, I was not going to be softened by these small concessions of cruel people. Stevie I supposed to be in a bewitched sleep, like the poor princess, and I was determined to save him. I did not blame nurse. I imagined she was down-stairs in enchanted slumber too. I would save her afterwards.

After calling passionately on Stevie, touching his face, which was colder than stone, I slipped my hands over him down the sides of the box, nearly toppling in myself in the energy of labour.

I see myself now, with pursed lips and frowning brows, panting in the extremity of haste. At last my hands met under the poor narrow shoulders, and I proceeded to drag the body out of the box.

I had nearly accomplished the feat, and Stevie's head and one arm hung over the side, when the door opened and my stepfather stood upon the threshold, dazed with horror, I can now believe. His look so terrified me that I clambered down from the chair, with an inclination to cry.

"What have they done to Stevie?" I gasped, as I saw him gently lift back the dark head and desecrated limb.

My stepfather's eyes brimmed over, and he took me into his arms, murmuring vague words about heaven and angels, with his wet cheek pressed upon mine. This was how I learnt that Stevie was dead.

Chapter IV. THE LAST DAYS OF HAPPINESS.

After the vivid impression of Stevie's death, the days are a blank. Memory only revives upon a fresh encounter with my kind.

A little boy, a friend of my parents, was sent down to nurse's to gain strength by a first-hand acquaintance with cows' milk and the life of the fields. Louie was an exciting friend. He had the queerest face in the world, like that of an old and wrinkled baby's, for mouth a comical slit, and two twinkling grey eyes as small as a pig's. His hair was white, and he grinned from morning till night, so that, like the Cheshire cat, he rises before me an eternal grin.

He taught me a delightful accomplishment, which afforded me entertainment for several months—the repetition of nursery rhymes. He possessed a book of this fanciful literature, and his private store as well was inexhaustible.

We spent a day of misery together once because he could not remember the end of one that began—

"There was an old man who supposed The street door was partially closed."

For nights I dreamed of that old man, and wondered and wondered what happened because of his error about the street door. I beheld him, grey-haired, with a nightcap on his hair, with a dressing-gown wrapped round him and held in front by one hand, while the other grasped a candle, and the old man looked fearfully over his shoulder at the door. I must have seen something to suggest this clear picture, but I cannot tell what it was.

Sometimes his face underwent all sorts of transformations, resembled in turn every animal I had ever seen and several new monsters I was unacquainted with. The eyes changed places with the mouth and the ears distorted themselves into noses. Before I had done with him, he had become quite a wonderful old man.

Our great amusement was to repeat the rhymes in a way of our own invention, taking turns to be chief and echo. This was how we did it:—

Louie. "There was an old man of the *Angela.* Hague *Louie.* Whose ideas were extremely *Angela.* vague. *Louie.* He built a *Angela.* balloon *Louie.* To examine the *Angela.* moon, *Louie.* This curious old man of the *Angela.* Hague."

My passionate admiration of the courage of the young lady of Norway made me always insist on taking the principal part when it came to her turn. The neighbors used to drop in of an evening, and add the enthusiasm of an audience to our own. They were specially proud of me as almost native-grown, and my eagerness to show off the attractions of the young lady of Norway generally resulted in my suppressing Louie's final rhyme. This was what we made of it:—

Angela. "There was a young lady of *Louie.* Norway *Angela.* Who occasionally sat in the *Louie.* doorway; *Angela.* When the door squeezed her *Louie.* flat, *Angela.* She exclaimed, 'What of *Louie.* that?' *Angela.* This courageous young lady of *Louie.* Norway."

Poor Louie, I learnt years afterwards, went to the dogs, and was despatched to the Colonies by an irate father. He was last heard of as a music-hall star at Sydney.

What sends bright and laughing children forth to a life of shame? Louie was the kindest little comrade on earth, unselfish, devoted, and of a tenderness only surpassed by my nurse's. Was this not proved when I began to droop and pine, missing the picture of Stevie kneeling on his sofa and staring out of the window?

I cannot say how long after Stevie's death it was before this want broke out as a fell disease. I worried everybody about the absence of that tragic face, and plied nurse with unanswerable questions. Neither Mary Jane nor the brindled cat, not even the applewoman and her tempting trays, nor the pond, nor my new terrier-pup that often washed my face, had power to comfort me.

I went about disconsolate, and was glad of a listener to whom it was all fresh, to discourse upon heaven and the queer means that were taken to despatch little children thither—an ugly box, when wings would be so much prettier.

Louie listened to me as I, with a burning cheek, told the roll of my sorrows and unfolded my ideas of the mysteries that surrounded me. Louie was not an intelligent listener, but he made up for his deficiency by an exquisite sense of comradeship. He would hold my hand and protest in the loudest voice that it was a shame, the while I suspect his mind ran on those nursery rhymes. But he loved me, there can be no doubt of that. I think he meant to marry me when we grew up.

I know when illness and a dreadful cough overtook me, he would let me lie on the floor with my head in his lap, while the exertion of coughing drew blood from my ears and nose. This too, he cried, was an awful shame.

I once saw him watch me through a convulsion with tears in his eyes, and I was immediately thrilled with the satisfaction of being so interesting and so deeply commiserated. It filled me with the same artistic emotion that followed my appreciation of the melancholy of my wordless singing.

Deep down in the heart of childhood—even bitterly suffering childhood—is this dramatic element, this love of sensation, this vanity of artist. So much of childhood is, after all, make-believe, unconscious acting. We are ill, and we cannot help noting the effect of our illness upon others. The amount of sympathy we evoke in grown-up people is the best evidence of our success as experimental artists with life. Even when we cower under a bed to weep away from our kind, we secretly hope that God or our guardian angel is watching us and feeling intensely sorry for us; and our finest conception of punishment of cruel elders is their finding us unexpectedly dead, and their being consumed with remorse for their flagrant injustice to such virtue as ours.

Who can limit the part as admiring audience a child condemns his guardian angel to play? For him, when humanity is cold and unobservant—as humanity too often is in the eyes of childhood—does he so gallantly play the martyr, the hero, the sufferer in proud silence. For his admiration did a little sister of mine once put her hand in the fire. She thought it was heroic, like the early Christians, and hoped her guardian angel would applaud, while common elders shouted in angry alarm.

Ah, never prate so idly of the artlessness and the guilelessness of children. They are as full of vanity and innocent guile and all the arts and graces as the puppies and kittens we adore.

How much, for instance, had the hope of praise and admiration to do with Louie's magnanimous kindness in that affair of the gipsies? I lay ill and exhausted from coughing on the sofa when he rushed in, panting with eagerness, to tell me that the gipsies had arrived over-night and were camped on the green, where they had a merry-go-round. I had never seen a gipsy, but Mary Jane had, and she often told me the most surprising things about them—how dark they were, how queerly they spoke, and how romantic they looked, like strange people in story-books. Of course I pined to see them, and the thought that I was chained to my sofa, when outside the world was all agog, and rapture awaited happier children upon the green, filled my eyes with tears.

I turned my face to the wall and wept bitterly. My heart was heavy with the sombre hate of Cain, and when I looked gloweringly at the blest little Abel by my side, he looked quite as miserable as my evil, envious heart could desire. His comic face underwent a variety of contortions before finally he made up his mind to blurt out an offer to forego the pleasures of the green, and stay with me.

But I was not a selfish child, and generosity always spurred me to emulation. Besides, I was already greatly comforted by the extent of Louie's sympathy, so I ordered him off to see the gipsies, and come back and tell me what a merry-go-round was like.

Still I did not mend, in spite of all nurse's care and tenderness, and it was decided to remove me to town. This was the decision of my stepfather, who was probably nervous since Stevie had dropped out of life in that quick and quiet way.

How well I remember the last day among all my dear friends! Mary Jane, Louie, and I, hand in hand, walked about all our favourite spots. The applewoman gave me an entire trayful of crab-apples, and wished I might come back with my rosy cheeks. I asked her to kiss me, and then she thrust a bun into my hand, and said huskily, "God bless you, my little lady!"

We went across to Mary Jane's, and I had a conviction that my heart was broken. I was going away into the land of the ogres and witches, and though I should probably be happy at last, since all things come right in children's tales, vague terror held me at the prospect of the unknown trials that awaited me. Mary Jane's mamma gave me raspberry vinegar and my tears mingled with the syrup. I asked to be let look once more at the views of New York, and then asked her if she would feel very sorry at my death.

They were still consoling me, and I was sobbing wildly in the arms of Mary Jane's mamma, while Louie relieved his stricken soul by protesting repeatedly that "it was an awful shame," when nurse and Jim Cochrane, in his Sunday clothes, came to carry me off to the car. All the village flocked to see me off, and breathed cordial love and benediction upon my departure.

Kindly Irish peasants, with their pretty speech and pretty

manners! Is there any other race whose common people can throw such warmth and natural grace into greetings and farewell? Big-hearted, foolish, emotional children, upon whose sympathetic faces, at their ugliest, still play the smiles and frowns, the lights and shadows of expressive and variable childhood. How they cheered and soothed me with their kind words, their little gifts, their packages of comfits and posies, a blue-and-white mug with somebody else's name in gilt letters upon it, and a tiny plate with a dog in a circle of fascinating white knobs.

This was the end of my brief sovereignty. Though of those old associations, for which I was destined to yearn so passionately many a year, memory may have become so dim as to leave only a trace of blurred silhouettes upon an indistinct background emerging from a haze of multiplied experience, I like to think that I owe to that bright start the humour and courage that have served to help me through a clouded life.

Chapter V. MARTYRDOM.

It would seem that happiness imprints itself more clearly and more permanently upon the mind than misery. Beyond a sense of enduring wretchedness, I can recall very little of my home life.

My sisters had a big play-room at the top of the house. Here they had ladders, which they used to rest in the four corners and climb up, pretending they were climbing up great mountains. They were much more learned than I in the matter of pretence and games. They knew all sorts of things, and could pretend anything. They had been to the pantomime, and could dance like the fairies. One of them had a brilliant imagination, and told lovely stories. In the matter of invention I have never since met her equal in children of either sex; but she was apt to carry experiment too far, for reading of somebody that hanged himself by tying a handkerchief round his neck and attaching it to a nail on the wall, she immediately proceeded to test the efficacy of the method upon the person of a pretty stepsister of four, whom she worshipped.

The child was beginning to turn colour already at the moment of rescue, and then followed the solitary instance of my stepfather's punishing one of us.

But my sisters were not kinder to me than my mother. I was an alien to them, and I loved strangers. They could not understand a sensitiveness naturally morbid, and nurtured upon affection. It was impossible that they could escape the coarsening influence of my mother's extraordinary treatment and neglect of them.

Left to grow up without love or moral training, cuffed and scolded, allowed illimitable liberty from dawn to dark, they were more like boys than girls. They never kissed one another or any one else. They were straightforward, honest, rather barbarous in their indifference to sentiment, deeply attached to each other under a mocking manner, vital, and surprisingly vivid and individual for children. There was not a particle of vanity or love of dress amongst the lot, though beauty was their common heritage. Their fault was that they never considered the sensibilities of a less breezy nature; that they were rough, unkind, for the fun of the thing, and could never understand the suffering they inflicted upon me.

One of their fancies, seeing how I shrank from hardness of touch or look or voice, was to teach me how to run away from a ghost.

It was a very high house, with several flights of stairs, and two of these inquisitors would take me between them, and tear me at a running pace down the whole length of stairs, my heels lifted from the ground, and only the tips of my toes bruised against each stair. At night I would go to bed aching with pain and terror, and sob myself to sleep, yearning for the faces and sights and sounds that had passed out of my life.

Ah, what tears I shed in that strange home! To have cried in childhood as I cried then, incessantly and for months, sometimes for the greater part of the day under a bed, that none of these mocking young creatures might see me and laugh at me; to have stood so intolerably alone among so many, without a hand to dry my eyes, a kiss to comfort me, a soft breast against which I could rest my tired little head and sob out my tale of sorrow,—this is to start permanently maimed for the battle of life. What compensation can the years bring us for such injustice? Could any possible future paradise make up to us for infancy in hell?

There are faces that stand out upon memory with some kindness in them for a pitiable little outcast. Chiefly, of course, my stepfather, who was as serviceably good to me as a man's unreasoning terror of a woman's temper permitted him to be. He saved me from many a cruel beating, and when I seemed more than usually miserable, he would, with an air of secrecy and guilt that charmed me, himself help to fasten on my hat and little coat, and carry me out upon his business calls.

They used to represent me to him as a dangerous small devil, describing my outbursts of fury but suppressing the provocation; and I once heard him exclaim angrily—"I am sick of these complaints of Angela's temper. When she is with me she is better behaved and gentler than any of them. You can twist an angel into a devil if you worry and ill-use it."

I know now that he suffered for his partisanship of me, and that he forsook my cause at last from sheer weariness of spirit and flesh. He thought it better for his own peace to leave me to the mercies of my mother, concluding probably that I should not be worse off.

Our home must have resembled the American man-of-war in the vicinity of which, the French Admiral wrote, nothing was heard from morning till night but the angry voices of the officers and the howling of trounced sailors. Up-stairs in their play-room the children were happy enough, but to venture down-stairs was the hardihood of mouse in the neighbourhood of lion. One or the other, for no reason on earth, but for the impertinent or irrational obviousness of her existence, was seized by white maternal hands, dragged by the hair, or banged against the nearest article of furniture. My mother never punished her children for doing wrong; she was simply exasperated by their inconceivable incapacity to efface themselves and "lie low." To show themselves also in her vicinity was an intolerable offence which called for instant chastisement.

Servants have been known to fly to the rescue. Once when I came home from a walk, one of the nurses complained in my mother's hearing that I had wilfully splashed my boots with mud. Instantly I was grasped, and the mystery to me to-day is how I survived such treatment. One of the servants, a delicate, fair young man, called Gerald, rushed up-stairs, scarlet with indignation, and tore me from my mother's hands. I have forgotten what he said, but he gave her notice on the spot in order to express himself more freely.

Once, again, I was rescued by a young lady in a silk gown of many shades. Her face is a blank to me, but I distinctly remember the green and purple lights of her shot-silk gown, and the novel sound of her name, Anastasia Macaulay. She had come to lunch that day, and had taken a fancy to me, which was quite enough to excite my mother. The scene is indistinct. I sat on Anastasia's lap, playing with her watch-chain, and suddenly I was on the floor, with smarting face and aching back. Anastasia saved me from worse. She sent me a picture-book and a doll, but never entered the house again.

Chapter VI. GRANDFATHER CAMERON.

The unhappiest little child that ever drew breath has immediate compensations between the dark hours undreamed of by elders. One of the persons that lent the relief of sparkle to those sombre months, and by whose aid I wandered blithely enough down the sunny avenues of imagination, which, like a straight road running into the sky, lead to Paradise, was my Scottish grandfather.

Grandpapa was a sombre-visaged little gentleman, not in the least like his formidable daughter. He had very dark eyes, and he often assured me that Stevie got his beautiful red-brown hair from him. I needed the assurance pretty frequently, for grandpapa's hair was white. He proudly drew my attention to the fact that there was not a bald spot, however.

In all ordinary matters of existence, grandpapa was of a happy facility. He tolerated every error, every crime, I believe, except a false note or an inferior taste in music. He loved me, not because of the accuracy of my ear, for I had none to speak of, but because of my instinctive passion for music. Still, in middle life, I can say there never has been for me a grief that could resist the consolation of music well interpreted.

If grandpapa found me in a corner white and dejected, he asked no questions,—he wished to be in ignorance of his daughter's domestic affairs, which was the reason, I suppose, he so sedulously avoided the society of my stepfather—but he took me off with him to hear music or singing somewhere. In winter he took me to the pantomime, and we sat in the pit, and he indulged me with an orange to suck.

In the Dublin season he took me to the Opera or the Opera-Bouffe with equal readiness. Sometimes there were morning or afternoon concerts, and I sat out with exemplary gravity sonatas and concerts or part-singing, and woke up to genial comprehension of the ballads and simple melodies.

Grandpapa had one great charm. He never spoke to me as a child, and I rarely understood the tenth of his talk. That was why, no doubt, as a personage grandpapa appealed so delightfully to my imagination. He was a mystery, a problem, a permanent excitement. A month or a year—perhaps, to be more accurate, a month—would elapse without my seeing him, and then suddenly he would again enter the chaos of dreams and visions, a smiling dark-eyed old gentleman, with a long black cloak flung round his shoulder and a slouched felt hat that left revealed his abundant white hair.

He would place a finger on his lip and say, "Hush!" so mysteriously, looking round the room. How well I, who lived in such fear of my mother's presence, understood that attitude and look.

I have since been assured that grandpapa was a harmless lunatic. If so, he made lunacy more attractive to a child than sanity.

"Hush! I have that to say to you, child, which common ears may not hear. These people call me Cameron. But, Angela, my real name is Hamlet. I was born at Elsinore. I will take you to Elsinore some day. It is far away in a country called Denmark. You yourself, Angela, look like a Dane, with your yellow hair and blue eyes. Come, there is a concert at Earlsfort Terrace. They play Bach. I will take you."

Could anything be more calculated to win a child's esteem and reverence than this assertion that the world knew him by a false name?—that he was really quite another person from the person they believed him to be? Then, what sonorous words, Hamlet, Elsinore! Denmark I liked less—it sounded more like an everyday place—but Elsinore was as good as a fairy-tale in its awful beauty.

I asked him if you went in a ship over the sea to Elsinore, as Mary Jane told me you went to America; and when he nodded and said "Yes," I got to imagine there was no common sunlight on the sea as the ship crossed it to Elsinore, but the lovely white light I had seen at the theatre when the fairies danced, and all the people in the ship wore beautiful garments of white and green gauze, and there was soft music all the way, and the water shone like silver.

What I could not understand was why I should be a Dane because my eyes were blue, when grandpapa's, who was so obviously more of a Dane than I, were black. But grandpapa always frowned, and an odd flame shot into his mild glance, if you asked him questions.

He gave you facts, and expected you to make what you could of them. He was unreasonably proud, I thought, of his Scottish blood, all the same. He was a Highlander, he said, while my grandmother, he explained contemptuously, was a Glasgow lass. My uncle Douglas, he added, favoured his side, while my mother was a blonde Ferguson. Pity it was an intelligent little girl like me did not take more after the Camerons; but I had my uncle Douglas's nose, and with a Cameron nose I need never fear the future.

This was surely an excess of faith on my grandfather's side not justified by experience. He had been only saved from the poorhouse by a thrifty and judicious if hard-hearted wife, while my splendid uncle Douglas, with his curly head of Greek god, had wandered from debt through every expensive caprice, and was drowned sailing a little pleasure-boat on one of the Killarney lakes at the inappropriate age of twenty-four.

The Cameron nose has done as little for his young brother, my uncle Willie. I have always loved the image I have made to myself of my boy-uncle Willie, chiefly, I suppose, because of his brilliant promise and early death; but largely, I believe, because not only grandpapa Cameron, but others who remember him, tell me I resemble him in character and feature.

They say it was his death, coming so soon after the blow of uncle Douglas's doom, that turned my grandfather's brain. Willie had been articled to a well-known architect, who, being musical like my grandfather, was interested in his musical friend's bright-faced and witty lad, with about as much knowledge of music as a healthy puppy. This lamentable deficiency, however, brought about no disastrous clash between master and pupil.

The distinguished architect loved Willie Cameron for his good-humour, his industry, his quickness, and his impromptu jingling rhymes. He made everything rhyme with a delicious comic absurdity, even the technical terms of his profession, and in consequence no one was jealous of the master's preference for his funny Scottish pupil. You see, he was so much more of an Irish than a Scottish lad. Born on Irish soil, he seems to have inherited the best of native virtues, and was universally beloved. Even his eldest sister, who never sinned on the side of tenderness, could not speak of uncle Willie without a smile.

So there were universal congratulations when Willie, barely of age, got his first commission. No one accused the architect of favouritism, though the first commission of a son could not have been of greater moment to him. Uncle Willie posted triumphantly off to the country, and the master told him to telegraph for his presence in the event of doubt or difficulty. The season was wet, and uncle Willie reached his inn that night drenched and shivering. They put him into damp sheets. The next day was no drier, and uncle Willie drove off on a car in the rain. It was his last drive alive. Ten days later what remained of him was driven to the cemetery amid plumes and crape and white flowers.

It was curious that while grandpapa Cameron was always ready to speak of his handsome son Douglas, of Willie, whom he loved best, he only spoke to me once,—that was when he showed me an indefinite boy's picture, and curtly told me it was my uncle Willie's portrait, and added, dreamily, that I was the only one of his grandchildren who resembled Willie.

That fact, perhaps, had more to do than my musical proclivities with his preference for me. He would give me five-shilling pieces from time to time, and beg me "not to mention it." I took the pieces gratefully, pleased with their brightness and largeness; but I own I found pennies more useful. A child can buy almost anything for a penny, but the only use of a silver five-shilling piece seemed to me to be able to look at it from time to time. Had I known anything of arithmetic, I might have calculated how many pennies were contained in these big silver pieces, and have changed them for an inexhaustible store of my favourite coin.

But I was not clever enough to think of this, and by the time I was sent across the sea to school in Warwickshire a year later, I had as many as six five-shilling pieces in a box, which then did stout service in supplying cakes and sweets on the scarce occasions I was allowed to make such needful investments.

Grandpapa Cameron lived in a little cottage out of town, with a long back-garden, where he spent his time cultivating roses. He had a disagreeable old cook and a red-nosed gardener, and he saw no society but a couple of priests, who took it in turn to drop in of an evening to play cribbage.

On Sunday he went to the one church where Mozart's and Beethoven's masses were sung. Once a new hardy organist with a fanciful French taste introduced Gounod.

My grandfather's face changed. He cocked an indignant ear, turned abruptly in his seat facing the altar, and looked long and angrily up at the choir. The horrid and sentimental strains of Gounod continued, and, unable to bear it any longer, my grandfather clapped his hat over his eyes, with a disregard for the religious prejudices of his neighbours no less brutal than the new organist's disregard for his musical sensibilities.

He walked out of church, and meditated upon his protest for a week. When I mention my belief that my grandfather had only become a convert from Scottish Presbyterianism to Roman

Catholicism because of Mozart's and Beethoven's masses, it will be recognised what a desperately serious matter for him was this impertinent introduction of light French music into church.

He succeeded in gathering a cluster of musical maniacs, one of whom was his friend the distinguished architect. The four planted themselves, with arms folded and furious purpose in their eyes, not in the least like Christians come to Sunday prayers, but like heroes bent upon showing an uncompromising front to injury. They heard in silence the opening roll of the organ, then the thin sweetness of Monsieur Gounod's religious strains filled the church, and the faithful sat up to listen to the Kyrie Eleison.

A distinct and prolonged hiss burst from the lips of the four musical maniacs, and my grandfather began to pound his stick upon the floor with an eloquence that left no one in doubt as to how he would treat the organist's head if he had it within reach. The officiating priests glanced round in surprise and astonishment. People rubbed their eyes, and wondered if they were dreaming.

There sat the four maniacs, hissing, booing, knocking their sticks on the floor, and "ohing" as they do in the House of Commons. Surprise was effaced in consternation, and a priest came down to the miscreants from the altar.

"Let that fellow stop his French nonsense and we'll stop too," shouted my grandfather. "I've been coming to this church for the past twenty-five years, and during that time have paid bigger fees than any of my neighbours. Why? Because there was a decent feeling for music here. Because you respected yourselves and gave us the best. But if you're going to degrade yourselves and follow an ignoble fashion and adopt French fads—well, sir, I swear I'll wreck the church—I will indeed."

The fight ended in my grandfather's defeat, and he never put his foot again into church. He carried his indignation so far as to insult an old French acquaintance, Monsieur Pruvot, the manager of a large wine house. Still sore upon the triumph of Gounod, he was accosted affably by Monsieur Pruvot, who cried out to him, waving his hat—

"How do you do, my dear Monsieur Camerone?"

"My name's Cameron, and I'm Mister, none of your damned French Monsieurs, Mr. Pruvot," roared my grandfather, pronouncing the mute *t* of the Frenchman's name with a vicious emphasis.

It is easy to imagine the amazement of the Frenchman, in ignorance of the Beethoven-Gounod episode, and who until then had always found my grandfather a genial and inoffensive neighbour. He made, by way of insinuating concessions to wrath, a complimentary remark upon "this charming little town of Dublin," pronouncing it in the French way.

"We call it Dublin, sir. Yes, I've no doubt it is a finer town than your native Bordox. I see no reason, sir, why we in Dublin should treat your town with a courtesy you, residing here, deny ours. If you can't learn to say Dublin, we may well decline to say Bordeaux. A very good morning, Mr. Pruvot."

Poor grandpapa Cameron! This was his last battle on earth, either in the interests of Beethoven or Dublin. A few days later he was found in bed with his face to the wall—dead.

Chapter VII. PROFILES OF CHILDHOOD.

The flow of the day in my city home is lost for me. But pictures and portraits stand out, sometimes blurred, sometimes surprisingly distinct, upon a confused background. There was food enough for curiosity and dreaming in the pauses of suffering. I must have lived for several days in an enchanted world solely by the single glimpse I had of my godfather.

He had sent me a present of a book about cocks and hens, largely illustrated. I was sitting in the store-room poring over it in the dreary society of Mrs. Clement, the new housekeeper. The previous one, Mrs. Dudley, I remember vaguely as a stern unsympathetic person, with crimped iron-grey hair under a voluminous cap trimmed with puce ribbons. She once forced me to swallow a Gregory-powder in a delusive snare of black-currant jam. I must have swallowed medicines before and since, and yet the taste and smell and look of that nauseous powder are still with me whenever my mind reverts to those days. Hence my delight when I learned that Mrs. Dudley was going away, and my cordial welcome of her successor, Mrs. Clement.

"So she's in here," somebody cried, rapping with a stick upon the door ajar.

I looked up from my book and saw a wonderful sight, of which I was afterwards vividly reminded in a French school by a picture of the famous "Postillon de Longjumeau," a jaunty figure with a pointed black beard and a tall wide-brimmed hat on one side. He bore himself gallantly, wore top-boots, a long coat with several little capes to it, and carried a smart riding-whip in his hand. This was my godfather.

I had never seen him before, and to my lasting regret I have never seen him since. He was out in '48, was proscribed, and had wandered about strange lands. He died in China, having first sent my mother a pretty case of Imperial tea, which she distributed in minute portions to all her friends, measuring the tea out with a small silver egg-cup. As fast as each consumed her portion, she returned for another, and as my mother had always a greater pleasure in giving than in receiving, my godfather's present was soon exhausted.

I remember being swung up in the air and shrieking in pretended fright, for children, sensational and dramatic little creatures, must persuade themselves there is an element of peril and adventure in their tamest diversions. Not to imagine oneself afraid is to miss the peculiar zest of enjoyment.

When I was seated gravely on his knee, my godfather asked me to spell out a few lines of his book.

"Cocks and hens—eh? Just suit a little girl from the country," he laughed, helping me to hold the book.

"I had a little dog at Mamma Cochrane's. I liked it better than cocks and hens," I protested meekly.

"Wants a dog now, does she? Queer little woman! She's still too pale, Mrs. Clement, much too pale and thin. Fretting for her Mamma Cochrane, I suppose. Well, I'll see if I can't get her a nice dog with curly hair, that'll cry 'Bow-wow' when you pull its tail. Know where China is, missy?"

I had heard of a china doll, and my Mamma Cochrane had two beautiful black-and-white china dogs. I supposed at once that China was a land where the dogs and dolls were all of china, and I wondered if the people were of china too. My godfather laughed as only a big man with a beard seems to be able to laugh. I was sure you could hear him down in the hall and up in the nursery. It was very comforting, that loud laugh, and I became instantly communicative, and told him all I knew about America and New York. He said it took a much bigger boat to go to China, which was farther off than New York, and that there were crocodiles in the rivers that ate men, and there was so much sunshine that the people were quite yellow.

After that, whenever it was unusually sunny, I was safe to astonish somebody by saying I supposed it was always like that in China. Somehow, the image of my jovial godfather was melted in a great glare of yellow light, through which yellow faces came and went, up and down long rivers, where unknown monsters, understood to be crocodiles, tossed about in a ruthless quest of man.

Mrs. Clement, the housekeeper, is another portrait that stands out in luminous relief from a crowd of unremembered faces. Her dress was seemingly as unalterable as a uniform. It consisted of a black silk gown, very wide at the base and gathered in at a slim waist, a white lawn fichu trimmed with delicate lace, and fastened with a gold brooch containing the features of a young man with a dark moustache.

I never dared to ask her who the young man was. She was

kind to me, but she kept me at arm's-length by her terrible sadness, and infant curiosity was the last thing she encouraged. Her face was pale, her thin yellow hair was pale, and her blue eyes were pale. Those faded hues suited the melancholy of her smile and regard.

Seeing me persecuted and unhappy, she took me under her protection, and would let me sit for hours at her feet in the storeroom, while she mended linen.

I read to her, and when I was tired of reading I told her stories of my past. Like grown-up mourners, it relieved me to talk of my sorrow and describe the paradise down there beside the pond and the applewoman's stall.

She listened with mild interest, and I was not so engrossed in my own troubles as not to remark the sadness of Mrs. Clement. The children up-stairs were sure she had committed some dreadful murder, and was brooding in remorseful reminiscence. They did not like her, because she once scolded them for their treatment of me; but nothing they could say would induce me to think ill of my melancholy friend, and I continued to sit at her feet and watch her in wonder and awe.

Her niece Eily came into our service shortly afterwards. She had a beautiful fresh face like a wild-flower, made up of sweet dark-blue eyes, a blossom of a mouth, and morning hues upon her cheek. She was a girl made to beguile sense and sternness, and transform the lion to a lamb. Everybody immediately loved her, she had such a delicious way of saying "Ah, sure!" and lifting up a pair of the most Irish of eyes in bewitching appeal.

My parents adopted her as a sort of daughter, and a mere hint of a lover at her heels was enough to wake the Quixote in my stepfather. They married her afterwards to a promising young Englishman, my father giving her away and my mother supplying the trousseau.

The Englishman was so enamoured of all things Irish that he gave the most flagrantly Hibernian names to his children, in opposition to Eily's romantic tastes, who adored every out-of-the-way name of fiction. When I met them, years afterwards, his affected drawl and pretty suspicion of lisp managed to give a foreign charm to our common name "Paddy," by which the eldest boy was called.

Eily's face was just the same wild-flower, a little faded and drawn, and "Ah, sure!" was still on the tip of her tongue in all the beguiling glamour of Erin. But what a sad change! Tears looked fatally near the surface, and the smile was deprecating and anxious.

She had fallen from petted servitude into troubled servitude, and longed for the clatter of her aunt's household keys among the linen and china and preserve-presses of the storeroom. She longed for my stepfather's cheery "Well, Eily, little puss," and instead had to listen to an exacting husband's complaints of her deficiencies as housekeeper and sick-nurse. He had married a bird, and grumbled incessantly because it lacked the solid capacities of a cow.

"And your aunt, Eily?" I asked.

"Poor aunt died long ago. She never recovered the death of her only child, Frank, who was drowned going out to America."

So the young man in the brooch was Mrs. Clement's son, after all, and her melancholy, that had so puzzled my childhood, was not the gloom of remorse but the stamp of a common bereavement.

By the side of my grandfather's avenue of rose-trees ran a neighbour's garden. My grandfather was on nodding terms with his neighbour; but there sometimes came a bright-faced lad with a flaxen down upon his upper lip. His name caught my fancy, and I thought a fairy prince could not have a finer one. It now represents to the world a figure so very different from the vague but pleasant profile memory likes to dwell upon, that I permit myself to doubt if that kind boy and the O'Donovan Rossa of New York can be the same person.

The stripling I recall seems to me to have been eternally singing or whistling. I specially remember one song he was fond of—"Love among the Roses."

He would look across the low hedge and sing out, "Where's my little wife?" I kept it as a delightful secret from all the world that I was married to a boy called O'Donovan Rossa. The world is a cold confidant in such delicate matters, and has a way of looking as if it did not take little children seriously.

But O'Donovan Rossa had a little sister of his own whom he loved devotedly, so he knew all about little girls and their ways, and appeared to understand my conversation. So few grown-up people do understand the conversation of children, and children know this.

He would spring over the hedge just like a mythical

personage, and tumble unexpectedly on the grass-plot beside me, and my daisy-chains were matter of absorbing interest to him. Then what stories he had about blue dragon-flies, humming-birds, and bewitched crows! You may imagine if I looked forward to visits to grandpapa Cameron's cottage, with such a prospective attraction.

I did not disdain the rougher friendship of Dennis, my grandfather's gardener. He was a cheery individual with a very red face. He once gave me an orange and a penny when I arrived with cheeks and eyelids swollen from crying, with a conviction that I could bear my sorrows no longer. I ate my orange, and suddenly the world seemed brighter, and when I went off alone to purchase a pennyworth of crab-apples at a fruit-shop hard by, I began to take pleasure at the thought of to-morrow.

I was further consoled by one of grandpapa's shining five-shilling pieces, and then Dennis called me to fetch him a tool, shouting, "Look sharp now, and do something for your living," and I was so enchanted that all sense of desolation and ill-usage left me.

It is so easy to make a child happy that it is a mystery to me how the art is not universal with grown-up persons.

Among the blurred memories of days so remote is a ball given in the big town house. The excitement could not but reach us up-stairs beneath the stars. The nurse and housemaid were equally aflame, and stood watching the guests from the corner of the topmost landing, that commanded a glimpse of the drawing-room lobby. The rustle of silk and the sort of perfumed chatter that belongs to gatherings in full dress reached us, broken and vague like the beautiful fancies of dreams. Our little feet pattered with yearning to be down below in the thick of social pleasures, and we shouted out our recognition of each side face as a guest crossed the lobby. It was not the brilliant assortment of silks and satins and laces, the gleam of jewelled array, or the chatter that intoxicated me; it was the first blast of music that rolled up to us, and the penetrating charm of the fiddles.

I was always less looked after than the others, and watching my opportunity, I slipped down-stairs in my nightdress; I felt I must hear those fiddles nearer, and see how people looked when they danced. Mrs. Clement saw me a few steps above the drawing-rooms, and wanted to carry me back to bed; but I prayed so hard for one look, that she took me into her arms, and, skirting the lobby, went in on tip-toe to the cardroom, at the top of the drawing-rooms, where several persons were playing at little tables. Some of the guests looked up at the melancholy lady in black silk with the little child in its night-dress, staring in bewilderment at them. But Mrs. Clement placed her finger on her lips, and they smiled at me and continued their play.

They were playing "Il Bacio," and even now I can never hear that tinkling waltz without a throb. It brought tears to my eyes then, and all night it formed the accompaniment of my dreams. The only couple I clearly saw in that paradise of colour, light, scent, and sound was my stepfather, who whirled past us with a tall dark girl in amber satin, who was smiling most radiantly as she danced.

This girl springs into my pictures of childhood in an odd inconsequent way. She was very handsome, of the sparkling brunette type, with white teeth, and hard bright eyes as black as the hair that rippled low down on either temple, and was caught under the ear in an old-fashioned bunch of ringlets. She was under my mother's protection, who was very kind and generous to her, having an inscrutable liking for strangers,—above all, needy strangers. She was a woman to turn her back inevitably upon a friend in prosperity, and court him in poverty. There was nothing of the snob in my mother, I must admit.

Another vivid picture I have of this young girl is a gloomier and more impressive one. I cannot tell why I was chosen for that drive. I suppose it was because I looked so delicate and unhappy that my stepfather insisted on having me. He drove a pair of spirited horses, and I sat opposite my mother and the dark young girl. She did not smile once that day, and the extreme sadness of her face riveted my attention. I thought I had never seen any one so beautiful and interesting, and I wondered why her eyes kept continually filling with tears.

She and my mother whispered mysteriously from time to time, and the disconnected words that reached my ears were no enlightenment for my puzzled brain. Ordinarily I was too dreamy or too excited to have much curiosity for my fellows. I preferred my own thoughts to speculations upon creatures so dull and undiverting as big people. But this day it was different. A brilliant young lady in long dresses, with a glittering ring upon her finger, whom my parents treated with every kindness and consideration, could be just as miserable apparently as a small neglected girl. It was truly a wonderful discovery.

We drove along the Kilmainham road, I now know, and as we went farther north, the pretty girl's tears flowed more freely, only she did not cry as we children cry. She bit her lips, and every moment thrust her handkerchief angrily into her eyes. My mother seemed to scold her for having wished to come that way, and I thought wanted to divert her attention from something the girl was evidently anxious to see.

We stopped near a large building, and there was my stepfather turned towards us and talking a strange jargon. From dint of puzzling over each word, I arrived at the extraordinary conclusion that somebody this young girl loved was in prison, that it was not wicked apparently to be locked up in prison, and that the woodwork they were gazing at, my stepfather with his hat in his hand, was something bad men were getting ready for her friend's destruction. The young girl stared up at the woodwork with streaming passionate eyes, and then buried her face in her handkerchief, and rocked from side to side in a dreadful way. We were driving on, and I gazed up to see what my stepfather was doing. He, too, was wiping away tears, and his hat was right down upon his eyes.

The mystery was solved years afterward. This girl was engaged to a political prisoner recently condemned to death. My mother used to take her to see him at Kilmainham Jail, and she had insisted on being driven round by the prison the day before the execution.

My grandmother lies farther back, a fainter picture in that world of unsatisfactory grown-up people. While she lived, her favourite present to each of her granddaughters was either a grey or green silk dress, with a poky bonnet and ribbons to match. In the grey we must have looked like little Quakeresses, and in the green like a gathering of the "gentle people" out of the moonlit woods, our proper dominion.

Her I remember indistinctly as a thin-lipped, unpleasant-looking woman, who had a fixed opinion that children must either be "saucy" or "bold." I was bold, because I was always too frightened of her to say anything, saucy or meek.

She used to lie in bed or on the parlour sofa, sipping egg-flip and reading religious books. She was very devout; but her religion, I suspect, served neither to brighten her own nor any one else's life. It had a sombre, vinegary aspect, more concerned with punishment due than pleasure merited, more attuned to severity than Christian mildness.

By some unaccountable process she melted out of my existence, having darkened it for some months, from which I infer that her death passed unnoted by me or was not explained to me. I did not see her dead, and can record no gentle deed of hers living. She never kissed me, but sometimes shook my hand in a loose gentlemanly fashion, and exhorted me not to be so "bold."

Once she nearly broke my heart. The cook had made some damson jam, and while I was alone in the parlour turning over the leaves of one of grandpapa's music-books, which looked so mysteriously wonderful to me, she carried in a specimen bowl, and left it on the table with some loose coppers. I still see that bowl. It was white, and had a wreath of pink roses.

When I tired of my music-book, I wandered by a natural impulse into temptation. The bowl was out of my reach, but I soon remedied that by drawing over a chair and climbing upon it. I dipped my finger into the bowl, and then put it into my mouth. It tasted, as indeed I fully anticipated, good. You may imagine the alacrity with which I continued the operation, without any heed of the blotches of jam that dropped upon the table.

Both the hall-door and parlour-door were open, and I heard loud sobbing. I was acquainted with sorrow myself, which was a reason I never heard a child's cry unmoved. I slipped off my chair, and ran out into the hall.

A ragged little follow sat on the doorstep, crying as if his heart would burst. I raced down the steps, and sat by his side to comfort him. He had cut his foot, and I asked him if it would not hurt less if he had some apples to eat. Crab-apples always soothed my own immeasurable woes and lightened the pangs of solitude for me. The weeping boy looked at me sullenly, and nodded.

In I flew again and came out with the coppers grasped in my jammy palm, and holding the bowl of damson jam tightly wedged between my pinafore and both hands.

"There's splendid jam here," I said, and invited the sufferer to dip his finger into the bowl.

He did so, and stopped crying. He was quite consoled, and nearly emptied the bowl in the avidity of his appreciation. Then I gave him the coppers, and told him the name of the shop where he could get lots of the nicest crab-apples. The hall-door was still open, and the parlour was empty when I carried back the bowl. I left it on the table, and went out into the garden to talk to Dennis.

I had no idea of having done wrong. At nurse's I was free to take what I liked, and I was not at all familiar with the sin of stealing. Judge, then, my surprise when cook came out for me with a flaming face, and assured me I "would catch it." I stopped playing, and felt chill with apprehension. What was going to happen to me now? Grandpapa was not there to protect me, and I had not much faith in Dennis's power to save me.

Cook dragged me up-stairs, scolding me all the way. She called me a thief, a robber, and said I was worse than the dreadful highwaymen they wrote of in books. I whimperingly protested. I was not a thief, I cried indignantly; I was not a robber. I did not know what a highwayman was, but I was sure I was not that either.

"Ah! you'll catch it," was all cook deigned to reply.

How grossly and wickedly mismanaged children are by people who do not think or stop to study them! So many tears and tremors and moments of black despair, because angry and impatient persons will not take the trouble to use the right words and correct with justice and sense. To abuse an ignorant little child in disproportionate language, at an age when imagination exaggerates and magnifies everything, for an impulsive action and an inconsequent error, and tell her "she would catch it," is surely a hideous perversion of strength and power.

Relatively speaking, that moment was not less vivid and awful for me than the worst hour of a heretic in the days of the Inquisition. And I had as little faith in the justice or kindness of my judges as any wretch of those times.

My grandmother sat in bed with her glass of egg-flip in her hand, presiding relentlessly over my castigation. Again I was informed that my crime was an appalling one. I had robbed money and robbed jam. There was no softening of my grandmother's face when I said, through my sobs of terror, that I only took the money to give it to a little boy that had hurt his foot and was crying. Cook administered an unmerciful whipping, as if there were not beatings enough for me without cause down in the big town house I hated.

No, verily; there are times, when I look at happier children to-day and remember that poor unhappy little child of years ago, I feel there are wrongs we cannot be expected to forgive, scars no time can efface, blunders no after good will ever rectify. I could weep to-day as bitterly for that little child, so alone, so throbbing with untamed fears, as ever she wept for herself then.

Chapter VIII. REVOLT.

I do not know how long my martyrdom in the town house had endured before I resolved to make an end of it myself. Nor do I yet quite understand how the scene that led to an excess of misery so terminated began.

I had been more contented that day than usual. The nurse had let me sit by the nursery fire while she bathed and dressed the latest addition to our family circle, a baby boy with a pink wrinkled face. Compared with that gurgling morsel of humanity, I felt very wise and old indeed. After that the nursemaid came and took me on her knee, and while perched there she sang me a song. I slept in the next room, and was not often allowed into the nursery, or I am sure the nurse and nursemaid would have made life easier for me.

Then I wandered into the play-room, and here great doings were afoot. They were getting up a transformation scene. On the top of each ladder a little girl sat, representing a fairy, and in the middle of the room a small child lay with a white cloth about her. When somebody clapped hands she sprang up, caught her skirts in either hand, and began to dance as she had seen the fairies in the pantomime.

They were all in high spirits that day, and let me look on without snubbing or laughing at me. Like all creatures unaccustomed to much mercy, this small favour filled me with joy, and I expanded upon a whiff of social equality.

Children resemble dogs in their dislike of intruders, and to these young people I daresay I, with my sulky miserable face, pale and woe-be-gone from association with sorrow and from unassuaged longing for other days, was an unattractive enough intruder. One there was who always resented my appearance in their midst more than the rest, my mother's favourite, the five-year-old queen of the establishment. My mother used to call her queen, and tell her that she was at liberty to do what she liked to me, as I was only a slave.

What a surprising amount of good must lie at the bottom of a nature so trained, that it ever developed into good-natured and generous womanhood! But to expect that the child in those days should have been other than a little vixen to me, would be to expect the impossible.

The play was interrupted for dinner, and after dinner the troop marched up again to the play-room to resume their game. I stayed down-stairs, and stole into the storeroom to talk to Mrs. Clement. Near tea-hour she sent me on some message, and that, of course, was a proud moment for me. Children love to be sent on messages between their elders. They instantly become as inflated as a general's aide-de-camp, and hardly need a horse in imagination to place them in their own esteem above the level of other children.

How it all came about I know not. The queen and the slave encountered somewhere on the way. We met like two young puppies and snarled. The queen had a despotic notion of her own rights. She might snarl at me, but I had not the right to reply. If she struck me it was part of my punishment for being in her way, and my duty was to bear it.

I don't suppose she reasoned this way any more than the young puppy does when it flies at the throat of a mongrel it dislikes. Anyhow, she struck me. I was a proud, fierce little devil, and being two years her senior, I laid her low, with an ugly red stain on her white cheek.

As I do not remember how it began, so I do not recall how it ended. There is a dark blank of several hours—centuries it seemed to me—and I was in my cot sobbing myself to sleep, and telling myself that I could not bear it, and to-morrow would run away to my dear everyday parents.

Next morning I sullenly submitted to be dressed and taken down to breakfast. But the red-and-white bowl I ate my bread and milk out of no longer delighted my eye, and no amount of sugar could take the taste of bitterness out of that bread-and-milk. My stepfather came into the room, and looked at me in reproachful silence. Usually he kissed me and flung me up to the ceiling. But now that the poor miserable little worm had turned and struck the idol of the house, his own child, he had no kind word for me. He only knew of the affair what he had been told, and how many thoughtless big people can understand what goes on in the hearts of sore and lonely babies?

He may have noted the sadness of my face, but what did he know of the inward bruise, the hunger for love and sympathy, the malady of life that had begun to gnaw at my soul at an age when other little girls are out racing among the flowers in a universe bounded and heated and beautified by the love of mother and father?

Mrs. Clement must have been very busy, for she did not

come to comfort me. Perhaps she, too, thought I was a fiend. But I was too proud to seek to explain matters to any one. If they wanted to believe I was bad, they might think I was as bad as ever they liked.

In my open-worked pinafore and little house slippers, bare-headed and bare-armed, I stole anxiously down-stairs. The baker was carrying in the bread, and the hall-door was open. This was my chance, and I seized it. Ah, there were the wide long streets, and however cruel the big people might be who went up and down them, at least they could not hurt me, for I did not belong to any of them.

Like a frightened hare I scurried along the pavement until I came to a big crossing. I paused here in new peril. To go over alone meant to risk contact with the wheels and horses continually rolling and stamping by. I had not the courage to do this, and I stood gazing disconsolately across at the happy people walking so unconcernedly on the other side. While I stood there a policeman marched up in a leisurely fashion. He looked as if he might help a little girl, and I knew when robbers attacked you the proper person to assist you was a policeman.

"Please, Mr. Policeman, will you take me across the street?" I asked, going boldly up to him.

The amiable giant put out his hand, grasped my eager fingers, and I pattered along at his side as he gravely led me over the crossing. Without a word, I raced ahead; the quicker I ran, the quicker I believed I would reach Mamma Cochrane's house, and my dear friends, nurse, and Louie, and Mary Jane.

In what direction I ran I know not to-day; I seemed to have been running down interminable streets for hours and hours, till at last my feet in their thin slippers began to ache. Gradually my legs stiffened, and it was less and less easy to continue running. Nobody stopped me, but I have an idea many stared at me. I hardly knew which I most feared, to be overtaken and carried back to my mother, or to be let die of hunger in those big unfriendly streets. Either prospect seemed so terrible to me in a moment of lucid vision, that I at once dropped upon a doorstep and began to cry.

"What's the matter, little lady?" a tall policeman asked, with a smile of insidious kindliness.

"I want to find my everyday mamma so badly," I sobbed. "But it's so far away,—I'm very tired, and nobody is sorry for me, though I'm so unhappy."

I gazed anxiously up into the face of the big policeman, and wondered if such a very big person could possibly understand and pity the sorrows of such a very small person as myself.

"What's your name?" asked the big policeman.

"Angela."

"And where do you live, missy?"

"Oh, a dreffal long way off—in a big house down there," pointing vaguely in front of me, "in a horrid big house, without any fields or flowers at all."

"Won't you come along with me, missy?" coaxed the policeman, and if he had asked me to go to prison with that look and smile, I would cheerfully have gone, I think.

He lifted me into his arms and carried me, I know now, to the nearest police-station. Here I was installed upon an inspector's knee, and an army of giants stood round me and made much of me. How the gentlemen of the force may appeal to others, I know not, but I must ever regard them as my kindest friends. They petted me prodigiously, and vied with each other in providing me with luxuries. One held a piece of bread-and-jam for me, another a slice of bread-and-honey, and various hands held out sweetmeats and cakes and apples. The thing was to satisfy everybody and devour each delicacy successively.

The amiable giants smiled upon me, and appeared to listen to my confidential chatter with admiration and delight. Out of the gloom of the domestic circle I could be expansive to rashness. Between bites, I told them the tale of my private grievances, and they shook sympathetic heads over my account of Stevie's disappearance in a queer box, and dropped their jaws when I, charmed with the sensation I had made, assured them that I too was so miserable and lonely that I would like to be put in a box and sent to heaven. I would much rather go back to Mamma Cochrane's than anything; but if I could not find her I would like to die like Stevie, unless the policemen would take care of me and let me stay with them always.

The inspector was ready to adopt me on the spot; meanwhile, as I was tired and the excitement had worn off, he encouraged me to fall asleep on his knee, which I was nothing loath to do.

The rest is a vague memory. Somebody shook me, and I

opened my eyes and saw my stepfather smiling at me. I thought I was at home, and rubbed my eyes, and then sat up. But I was still in the inspector's arms—I recognised his black cap and grey beard. My circle of friendly giants had vanished; but on a table beside me were heaped unfinished slices of bread and jam and honey, gingerbread nuts, shrewsbury biscuits, bulls' eyes, brandy balls, sugar-stick, and apples. A couple of policemen stood at the door and grinned in eloquent assurance of continued friendship, and the inspector had not released his comforting clasp of my wearied body.

"Papa, I'm so happy here. Don't let us go back any more to Sunday mamma. Let us stay here always with the nice policemen."

My stepfather laughed his joyous cordial laugh, and caught me in his arms. He shook hands with the inspector and the policemen, and carried me into a cab. I was still too sleepy and tired to whimper, and we had hardly set off before I was fast asleep on my stepfather's knee.

Chapter IX. MY FRIEND MARY ANN.

Seven has been described as the age of reason. I am curious to know why, since many of us at fifty can hardly be said to have attained that rare and sublime period. John Stuart Mill, for his misfortune, at seven may have discovered some rudimentary development of sense, but no other child of my acquaintance past or present. But if seven is not marked for me by the dawn of reason, it is important as the start of continuous reminiscence.

Memory is no longer fragmentary and episodic. Life here begins to be a story, ever broken, ever clouded, with radiant hours amid its many sadnesses, quaint and adorable surprises ever coming to dry the tears of blank despair and solitude; an Irish melody of mirth and melancholy, all sorts of unimaginable tempests of passion and tears, soothed as instantaneously as evoked, by the quickening touch of rapture and racial buoyancy. Mine was the loneliest, the most tragic of childhoods, yet I doubt if any little creature has ever been more susceptible to the intoxication of laughter, more vividly responsive to every mirthful and emotional claim of life.

After my singular and enchanting experience of the police-station, where, as a rule, the hardened instruments of justice are not permitted to show themselves in so gracious and hospitable a light, it was decided to expatriate the poor little rebel beyond the strip of sullen sea that divides the shamrock shores from the home of the rose. There, at least, vagrant fancies would be safely sheltered behind high conventual walls, and the most unmerciful ladies of Mercy, in a picturesque midland town of England, were requested to train and guide me in the path I was not destined to adorn, or indeed to persevere in.

Pending the accomplishment of my doom, I was removed from the centre of domestic discord and martyrdom to the suburban quiet of my grandfather's house.

This decision had its unexpected compensation. The cross old cook, whom I had not seen since the day I stole her bowl of damson-jam, had disappeared to make way for Mary Ann, the divine, the mysterious, the sublime, the ever-delicious Mary Ann. Where did she come from, whither has she vanished, the soother of the sorrows of those most lamentable days?

Alas! now I know the secret of her enchantment, of those perishable surprises of mood and imagination that so perpetually lifted me out of my miserable self, diverted me in my tragic gloom, and sent me to bed each night in a state of delightful excitement. Mary Ann drank punch, and on the fiery wings of alcoholism wafted herself and me, her astonished satellite, into the land of revelry and mad movement. How ardently, then, I yearned for the reform of poor humanity through the joyous amenities of punch. Had my grandmother up-stairs consumed punch instead of her embittering egg-flip! Had the ladies of Mercy, my future persecutors, drunk punch, the world might have proved a hilarious playground for me instead of a desperate school of adversity.

Mary Ann possessed a single blemish in a nature fashioned to captivate a lonely and excitable child. She worshipped my uncle Lionel. My uncle Lionel was his mother's favourite—a Glasgow lad, my grandfather contemptuously defined him, without the Cameron nose; a fine, handsome, fair young fellow, the picture of my mother, extremely distinguished in manner and appearance, and reputed to be a genius. He is said to have written quantities of superlative verse which he disdained to publish; but as nobody ever saw even the manuscript, we may regard the achievement as apocryphal. He had finished his studies in Paris, which explained a terrifying habit, whenever he met me—frightening the wits out of me the while by his furious look—of bursting out into what I afterwards learnt to be an old French song: "Corbleu, madame, que faites vous ici?"

I wish grown-up persons could realise the shudder of terror that ran through me and momentarily dimmed for me the light of day, when I heard that loud voice, encountered the mock ferocity of that blue glance, and then felt myself roughly captured by strong arms, lifted up, and a shaven chin drawn excruciatingly across my tender small visage. These are trifles to read of, but what is a trifle in childhood? A child feeds greedily upon its own excesses of sensation, thrives upon them, or is consumed by them. To these early terrors, these accumulated emotions, these swift alternations of anguish and rapture, which made opening existence for me a sort of swing, perpetually flying and dropping between tears and laughter, from radiant heights, without transition, to pitch darkness, do I attribute the nervous illnesses that have so remorselessly pursued me in after-years. The wonder is the mind itself did not give way.

Big language for a handsome young man with a blonde moustache and an elegant figure to have provoked, with his Corbleu, madame! his theatrical fury, and his shaven chin. He now and then gave me a shilling to console me, which shilling I spontaneously offered to Mary Ann, whose real consolation it was, since it filled the steaming glass for her and my friend Dennis, the red-nosed coachman, and permitted me to sit in front of them, a grave and awed spectator of their aged frolics.

Immoral undoubtedly, yet that evening bumper of punch converted Mary Ann into a charming companion. She and the fire in front of us—for it was on the verge of winter—cheered me as I had not yet been cheered since I had left my kind Kildare folk. The tyrants sat above in state, while I, enthralled below, listened to Mary Ann, as she wandered impartially from legend to reminiscence and anecdote, and not infrequently burst into song and dance.

Her sense of hospitality was warm and unlimited. Dennis she welcomed with a "Troth an' 'tis yourself, Dennis, me boy." For me she placed a chair opposite her own, and sometimes, in the midst of her enjoyment, stopped to help me to a spoonful of the stimulating liquid from her tumbler, remarking with a wink that it brightened my eyes and considerably heightened my beauty. It certainly made me cough, sputter, and smartened my eyelids with the quick sensation of tears, and then she would meditatively refer to the days when she too was young, and had pink cheeks and eyes the boys thought were never intended for the salvation of her soul. I was a curious child, and was eager for an explanation of the dark saying, on which Dennis would chuck my chin, with the liveliest of sympathetic grimaces across at the irresistible Mary Ann, which made the saying darker still, and Mary Ann would fling herself back in her chair convulsed with laughter.

"Ah, Miss Angela, 'twas the devil of a colleen I was in thim days, most outrageous, with a foot, I tell ye, as light as thim cratures as dances be moonlight. Sure didn't I once dance down Rory Evans in the big barn of Farmer Donoghue's at Clonakilty, when there was that cheering, I tell ye, fit to lift the roof off the house."

At this point she invariably illustrated the tale of her terpsichorean prowess in a legendary past by what she called "illigant step dancing," and endeavoured to teach me the Irish jig. She observed with indulgent contempt that I showed a fine capacity for the stamping and whirling and the triumphant shout, but I failed altogether in the noble science of "step dancing."

But what I preferred to the dancing, exciting as it was, were the ghost-stories, the legends of banshees, the thrilling and beautiful tales of the Colleen Bawn and Feeney the Robber. Those two were for long the hero and heroine of my infancy. Gerald Griffin's romance she, oddly enough, knew by heart. I forget now most of the names of the persons of the drama, but at seven I knew them all as dear and intimate friends: the forlorn young man who wrote those magic lines, "A place in thy memory, dearest"—did even Shelley later ever stir my bosom with fonder and deeper and less lucid emotions than those provoked by those tinkling lines, breathed from the soul of Mary Ann upon the fumes of punch?—the perfidious hero who once, like Mary Ann, drank too much and danced a jig when he ought to have been otherwise engaged, Miles, Anne Chute, and the lovely betrayed Eily.

I knew them all, wept for them as I had never wept for myself, and was only lifted out of a crushing sense of universal woe when Dennis produced an orange, which was his habit whenever he saw me on the point of succumbing under alien disaster.

Sometimes, to entertain my hosts, I would volunteer to warble my strange symphonies, and was never so ecstatically happy as when I felt the tears of musical rapture roll down my cheeks, when Dennis, by way of applause, always observed lugubriously—

"Ah, 'twas the poor master was proud indeed of her voice. 'She'll be a Catherine Hayes yet, you'll see, Dennis,' he used to say, 'or maybe she'll compose illigant operas.'"

Alas! I neither sing nor compose, and listen to the singing and the music of others with unemotional quietude. So many different achievements have been fondly expected of me, that I have preferred the alternative of achieving nothing. Better demolish a multitude of expectations than build one's house of the perishable bricks of a single one!

Preparations for my departure around me must have been going on, but I perceived nothing of them. I vaguely remember daily acquaintance with a dame's school in the neighbourhood, whither Mary Ann conducted me every morning. But remembrance confines itself to the first positive delights of a slate and pencil. Next to my own operas and Mary Ann's stories, I could conceive nothing on earth more fascinating than a certain slate, after I had arduously polished it, a slate-pencil, and leisure to draw what I liked on the blue-grey square. There were little boys and girls on the benches before and behind me, but I only see myself absorbed with my new pleasure, making strokes and curves and letters, and effacing them with impassioned gravity.

Chapter X. THE GREAT NEWS.

A grown-up young lady, with yellow ringlets, in a black-and-white silk dress, paid a visit to my grandmother one day, when I heard myself described as "bold and saucy,"—heaven knows why, since I never uttered a word in that formidable presence, and felt less than a mouse's courage if I but accidentally encountered those severe black eyes. The young lady offered to show me her dolls. I never cared for dolls, and I went without enthusiasm. It was my first glimpse of girlish luxury. The room in which her treasures were kept seemed to me as large as a chamber of the palaces of story. There were trains, carriages, perambulators, about two dozen dolls of all sizes, with gorgeous wardrobes; there were beds, bonnets, parasols, kitchen utensils, dear little cups; babies in long clothes, peasants, dancing-girls, and queens with crowns on their heads and long cloaks. The young girl was one of the many extinguishable flames of my uncle Lionel, destined, like Goethe, to sigh for one, and then another in sentimental freedom, and end in bondage of an execrable kind. She is blurred for me, but that palatial doll's chamber and all those undreamed-of splendours remain still a vivid vision, like the lovely pantomime, whither Dennis took me with his pockets full of oranges to suck between the acts. Oh, that bewildering paradisiacal sight of the fairies! the speechless emotions of the transformation scene! the thirst, the yearning, for short muslin skirts, and limelight, and feet twinkling rapturously in fairyland! The humours of the clown and the harlequin left me cold; for, being acquainted with the extreme tenderness of the human body through harsh experience, I could not understand the pleasure the clown found in continually banging and knocking down the harmless harlequin. Each unprovoked blow left me sadder and more harassed. I felt the old man must be very much hurt, and wondered why the audience seemed to enjoy his repeated discomfiture so hugely. But the fairy dancing was quite different. Here was an untempered joy that did not pass my comprehension. To be a fairy by night, and possess all the young girl's toys by day! This was the dream harshly broken by the appearance of my sisters, themselves demure little fairies in green silk dresses and poky green silk bonnets.

They lured me out among the dead branches, where the robins were dolefully hopping in search of crumbs, and exclaimed together: "Oh, Angela, wait till you hear the news!"

What news? Why, I was to go away, across the sea, which was always awfully wet, like the pond, only bigger and deeper. A ship, they said, was like those little paper-boats the boys used to make at Kildare, and you sat in it and rocked up and down, unless a shark came and ate you up. Somebody told them that the English were dreadfully proud, and thought no end of themselves, and looked down on the Irish.

"But you must stand up for yourself, Angela. Tell them your father was king of Ireland lots of hundreds of years ago, and that long ago, when the kings lived, all your cousins and brothers were red-cross knights."

"What were red-cross knights?" I asked, deeply impressed.

"Oh, they were men who wore long cloaks with red crosses on them, and rode about on steeds."

"What's steeds?" I breathlessly inquired.

"Horses," was the pettish answer; "only you know they go quicker than horses, and knights always preferred steeds. And they took things from the rich and gave them to the poor."

"What things?" I again asked.

"Isn't she stupid? I declare she knows nothing. Why, food and money and clothes, to be sure. They'll say the Irish are dreadful ignorant and stupid when they see Angela, won't they?"

A great deal more was of course said between four passionate and voluble children; but all I remember of that winter afternoon was the stupendous news that I was going away in a ship soon across the sea to a foreign land, where I should be submitted to insult, perhaps torture, because I was Irish, if I were not previously devoured by a shark—a creature the more terrible because of my complete ignorance not only of its existence, but of its general features; and the mention of a new animal was something like the menace of the devil: large, luminous, potent, and indistinct. I already knew through Mary Jane that there was a Queen who put Irish people into prison, and entertained herself by hanging them at her leisure, and that evening I startled Mary Ann out of her senses by asking her if it was likely I should be hanged in England like Robert Emmet. And then, in order that she should have a proper notion of the extent of my acquaintance with Robert Emmet, I stood in the middle of the kitchen, with my arms strenuously folded, my brows gathered in a fearful frown to reproduce the attitude of

Robert Emmet in the dock, as depicted in the parlour of Mary Jane's mamma.

"You know the English hanged him 'cause he was Irish," I explained, extremely proud to impart my information. "Mary Jane told me so. When I fell into the pond she cried, 'cause she was afraid the Queen would hang her too."

Mary Ann laughed till she wept, and then drying her eyes, vowed she would like to see "thim English" touch a gould hair of my head. "If thim monsthers as much as lay a hand on ye, darlint, you just send me word, and me and Dennis 'll soon come over and whack them all round."

Perfidious Mary Ann! She failed to keep this large and liberal promise when, in my sore hour of need, I indited an ill-spelt epistle to her from Saxon shores, and urged her to come and save me. I did not insist upon the whacking, I only entreated to be taken back to Erin. Probably the letter never reached her.

I think that it was immediately after this engrossing hour that I found Mary Ann sobbing over an open trunk in the lumber-room. "Your very own, alannah; look at the big white letters," she cried, and wiped her eyes in a new linen garment before pressing it into the box. "Thim monsthers can't say as you haven't chimmies fit for any lady of the land. Ye're to wear a black cashmere o' a Sunday, just as if all your relatives was dead. Did ye ever hear the likes?"

I certainly never did, for strange to say I had not worn a black dress after Stevie's death. I did not, however, dislike the notion. Black was not a hue with which I was familiar. Still musing on all the extraordinary things that were continually happening, and wondering whether the eventual climax of an uncertain career would prove the shark or the gallows, not, however, using this superb word in my reflections on the end of a little girl precariously balanced on the boards of existence, I found myself confronted with my terrible grandmother in a farewell interview.

She was propped up with pillows, and her eternal egg-flip was beside her on a little table, along with her prayer-book, her spectacles, her rosary, and her favourite novel, which I afterwards learned was "Adam Bede." My mind reverted then, and has since often reverted, to an abominable scene in that chamber I abhored. I had been noisy or disobedient,—raced down the passage, or refused to go to bed when uncle Lionel shouted to me from above the kitchen-stairs, probably stamping my foot with the air of a little fury, which was my sad way in those untamed days. With a Napoleonic gesture, my uncle caught my ear, and dragged me into the awful presence. Here he was solemnly ordered to fetch the knife-sharpener, which he did; heated it among the flames till it glowed incandescent scarlet; then, my grandmother looking fiendishly on, gathered me between his knees, held my mouth open with one hand, and approached it to my lips. Of course it did not touch me, but memory shrinks, a blank, into the void of terror.

The precise text of my grandmother's address I forget, but the nature of her harangue is unforgettable. She addressed me as might a magistrate a refractory subject about to be discharged from a reformatory. I was exhorted not to be bold, or bad, or saucy, to say my prayers, to tell the truth, not to thieve (oh! that damson-jam and those coppers), not to get caught again by the police; I was warned that I might drop dead in one of my violent fits of rage, and then I would surely go to hell; was adjured to learn my lessons, to respect my superiors, to break none of the Commandments, to avoid the seven deadly sins, learn the Catechism by heart, with the alternative of having my hair cut short and being sent to the poorhouse. She then held out her yellow hand, and placed a sparkling sovereign in my small palm.

"Don't lose it. There are twenty shillings in it, and in each shilling twelve pennies. Good-bye, and don't forget all I've said."

She shook my hand in her loose gentlemanly fashion, as if I were a young man going to college instead of a baby girl of seven about to be expatriated alone among strangers, in an alien land, for no conceivable reason but the singular caprice of her who had given me so ill a gift as life. It was the last time I saw my grandmother. I heard soon of her death with complete indifference.

"Polly was a jolly Japanese," sang my uncle cheerily, as he caught me up in his arms, and carried me down to the cab, on which Dennis had placed my trunk. Mary Ann was weeping on the steps. She handed me a bag of gingerbread and two apples, and told me I was not to be "down."

"'Tis yourself that's worth all the English that ever was born," she asserted, and I dolorously assured her that whatever happened, even if the Queen came in person to hang me, I would keep "up."

"That's me hearty," roared Dennis, holding the cab-door. "In with you, and do something for your living."

Uncle Lionel lifted me in, gave me a crown-piece, and to my astonishment kissed both my cheeks without hurting me. He stood on the pavement, handsome, smiling, and elegant, as the cab drove off with solitary, bewildered little me as surely a waif as any orphan. And waving his hand, he turned unconcerned on his heel.

Chapter XI. PREPARING TO FACE THE WORLD.

Was it six weeks or six months since I left that big town house, a disgraced and blighted little being? Time to a child is so unequal a matter. A month may seem a century, a year appear vaguer than a dream. Indeed, I have never yet been able to tell myself how long a space of time actually separated my good-bye to Kildare and my departure for England. Multiplied experiences combined to mislead me.

Simultaneously with the opening of the cab-door opened the big door of my stepfather's house, and a group of little golden heads showed in the dark frame. Feet and hands and voluble lips and eyes played together, and for a very brief while I enjoyed the sensations of a heroine.

This small world was excited prospectively at the thought of my coming adventures. I was soon to represent to them the unknown, the elsewhere, the eternal dream of "far fair foreign lands." Things were to happen to me that never yet happened to mortal. I was to be snubbed by and to subdue a haughty people. Perhaps if I did something extremely outrageous I should be put into prison, with chains round my feet and wrists. Pending which, I was to travel for several hours by land and several hours by water.

"She has come already," they shouted gleefully. "Oh, such a dreadful person, Angela! taller than papa, and the skin is quite tight round her eyes and mouth as if she couldn't laugh."

She was, indeed, an odd-looking woman, the jailer to whom my parents so unconcernedly confided me. Not unkind, but austere and grotesque in her black cap and long black veil. She had left a Tipperary village to become a lady of Mercy in the English convent, and to her was intrusted the care of my deported self. In religion her name was Sister Clare, and the impression she has left on me is that of an inoffensive policeman masquerading in woman's attire, with limbs too long for a decorous management of them, honest, cold blue eyes, and, instead of the vivid hues of life upon the lean cheek, discoloured parchment drawn without a wrinkle tightly over the high-boned impassible visage.

I had the bad taste to show fright upon sight of her lugubrious garb of postulant, and like the little savage I was, passionately declined her proffered kiss; but when my stepfather held me on his knees beside her, and spoke to her with his charming affability, I let myself be coaxed into equable endurance of the queer picture. I saw then that she was not dangerous. Indulgence lurked beneath the austere expression, and if the glance was cold, it was neither hard nor cruel.

Up-stairs in the nursery the hours passed tumultuously in a frenzy of discussion. Each little head was busy forging its theory of deportment and action in circumstances so strange and adventurous as those of a baby girl going out alone among the sharks and foreigners of a cold undreamed-of world. The immediate fear was that I should disgrace my land by my Kildare accent. My eldest sister contemptuously declared that I talked "just like that disgusting little girl with the oily black ringlets"; and the imminence of a shower at the abrupt reference to the dear and absent Mary Jane, so far away, so unconscious of my perils and terrors and importance, averted an outburst of indignation at the wanton insult cast upon her picturesque head.

It was regarded as an aggravation of my imperfections that I could not write, else I might have kept up the lively excitement of my departure by a raw account of my adventures. But by the time I should have mastered the difficult art of writing and spelling, I should probably have forgotten all my wonderful experiences, and they would have lost all interest in the story of my early travels.

If my mother had been an early Christian or a socialist, she could not have shown herself a more inveterate enemy of personal property. Never through infancy, youth, or middle age has she permitted any of her offspring to preserve relics, gifts, or souvenirs. Treasures of every kind she pounced upon, and either destroyed or gave away,—partly from a love of inflicting pain, partly from an iconoclastic temper, but more than anything from a despotic ferocity of self-assertion. The preserving of relics, of the thousand and one little absurdities sentiment and fancy ever cling to, implied something beyond her power, something she could not hope to touch or destroy, implied above all an inner life existing independent of her harsh authority. The outward signs of this mental independence she ever ruthlessly effaced.

And my desolation was great when I found the old wooden box I had brought up from Kildare empty of all my beloved little relics of a fugitive happiness and of yearned-for friends. Gone the mug with somebody else's name upon it, gone the plate with the little white knobs and the painted black dog, gone my book about cocks and hens, the gift of that vision of romance, my godfather, swallowed up radiantly in Chinese yellow. Gone, alas! Stevie's "Robinson Crusoe" and his knife, and every tiny possession of a tiny sentimentalist, whose heart was so famished for love and kind words and kisses, and clung the more eagerly for this to these poor trifles.

I sat on the floor beside my empty box, and refused to be comforted. These things were to have softened the rigours of exile, might have gone with me to the scaffold as sustainment and benediction, if I had the misfortune to rouse the ire of that mysterious being, the Queen, whom Mary Jane depicted as sitting on a high throne, with a crown on her head and a knife in her hand for the necks of the unruly Irish.

But I had nothing now to take to bed with me, nothing to hug and weep over, nothing to tell my sorrows to when the society and persecution of big people become intolerable. I stood, or rather sat, alone in a desolate universe, with the violated coffin of my regrets in front of me. Being worn out with all I had gone through that day, I probably fell asleep sobbing against the empty box, and night robbed me of any further sense of misfortune.

Chapter XII. AN EXILE FROM ERIN.

The next day I was too fully conscious of being the heroine of a sensational drama, to shed tears over my lonely and miserable self. The boat left the North Wall early in the morning, so that toilet, breakfast, farewells were a hurry, a scare, the suspension of feeling in stunned senses. I scarcely tasted tea, but I looked forlornly at the lovely red-and-white cups as big as bowls, which I still remember as a comforting joy to the eye.

All the children around me were stamping and shouting, running every minute between mouthfuls to see if the cab had come, if my box were in the hall, and read aloud the label, "Passenger to Lysterby by Birmingham," in awed tones. It seemed so wonderful to them that I should be described as "passenger" to anywhere. Not a tear was shed by anybody. Only war-whoops and joyous voluble chatter and thrilling orders that rang along the passage like the clarion notes of destiny. Elsewhere hearts under such circumstances might break. Here they only palpitated with delight in the unusual, and the whole party was filled with a like impatience to lead me in triumph down to the cab, not from a heartless desire to get rid of me, but for the grand dramatic instant of farewell. They greedily yearned to bundle me into the fatal vehicle, for the intoxicating novelty of waving their handkerchiefs to me from the doorstep as the cab drove off.

What might follow for me they did not take into account, having neither imagination nor tenderness to help them to look beyond a glowing moment. What would follow for them they were already perfectly aware of: a wild race up-stairs, and a whole entrancing afternoon devoted to discussing my departure, voyage, and probable experiences.

My stepfather took me up in his arms, kissed me on both cheeks with his cheery careless affection, and carried me down-stairs. My mother followed with a shawl, and a packet containing cold chicken, bread, cake, and milk.

In the hall the terrible postulant stood waiting for me, and met my scared look with a quick nod, meant to assure me that although her aspect might be that of an ogre, she could be trusted not to devour a little girl. My mother gave her the lunch and the shawl, and told her to keep me warm, as I was not yet recovered from the effects of whooping-cough. Through the open door I saw my box on the top of the cab, and it seemed as if hundreds of shrill young voices were shouting blithely to me, "Good-bye, Angela." Quantities of soft young lips strove to kiss me at once, and dancing blue eyes sparkled around me, and gave me the sensation of being already cast out of a warm circle where my empty place would not be felt, where no word of regret would ever be uttered for the unwelcome waif that called them sister.

Without a tear or a word, giving back their joyous "Good-bye" without sorrow or revolt, I carried my mumbed little heart into the cab, so alone that the companionship of the postulant offered me no promise of protection or sympathy, and I never once looked at my stepfather sitting opposite me.

So I began my life, and so has it continued. Some obscure instinct of pride compelled me to wave my handkerchief in response to excited waves of white from the pavement. I looked as if I did not care, and this was the start of a subsequent deliberate development of the "don't care" philosophy, which the good ladies of Mercy triumphantly prophesied would eventually lead me to perdition. To perdition it did not lead me, but to many private hours of despair and suffering, for which I could claim no alleviation in the support of my fellows, since I had chosen the attitude of defiance and "don't care."

Heaven knows how much I cared! what salt passionate tears I wept because I always cared a great deal too much. But this nobody knew. My pride was to pass for a hardened reprobate, and such were my iniquities and the ferocity of that same untamable pride that if I achieved success in nothing else, here my accomplishment could not be disputed.

I can hardly tell now what were my first definite impressions of a ship and the sea, for it is difficult to recall the time when either constituted a novelty for me. If there were truth in the theory of transmigration of the soul, mine ought to be a remnant of a sailor's, or a child's born at sea. The big vessel inspired me with no fears, but an acute sensation of delight. The ropes, the sailors, the shouting, the wonderful file of porters laden with trunks and portmanteaus, cases and boxes dropping into mysterious depths with such an awful suggestion of fatality, the triumphant assertion of our herded insignificance, the captain's air of deity upon the bridge above, the marvels of the cabins below, and the little perilous stairs one rather slid than walked down, and the rapture of climbing up again from the stuffy dimness into the grey brine-tasting air, to laugh aloud in the intoxication of fear as the ship rose and fell upon the swell of a choppy grey sea rushing into the river's mouth.

It was sad to be alone, to be going away at seven from one's land and home among unknown barbarians; but for one strange hour I was not to be pitied, so quivering with pleasure was this first taste of adventure. By-and-by I grew stunned and quiescent, and was glad to sit still, curled up in some pretty lady's lap, where my cheek rested luxuriously against soft, warm fur. But for the moment I was too eager to see everything, follow every curious movement with childhood's wide alert gaze, hear everything, understand everything.

My stepfather, like a big, good-natured man, humoured me, and we seemed to travel together hand-in-hand over an entire world, looking at all sorts of odd things, and listening to all sorts of odd noises. It was less beautiful, to be sure, but how much more interesting than the pantomime! I provoked a shout of laughter from a man in a greatcoat with a tremendous black beard, by clamouring to know where the sharks were. Before the answer could come, a bell rang sharply, and somebody sang out "All ashore!"

"Good-bye, Angy, and God bless you! Be a good child, now, and don't fret," said my stepfather, stooping to gather me to him, and there was a break in his voice I had once before heard, when he found me with dead Stevie in my arms.

I can imagine what a piteous little object I must have looked, so frail and fair and small, standing alone on the big deck, without a hand to clasp, a fond smile to encourage me, lips to kiss away my tears. But he was too much of the careless, good-tempered Irishman to allow unpleasant emotions to trouble him except in a vague and transient way. Now I know how he would blink away the sad vision, and as he turned from me with a cheery "Don't fret," he waved his hand encouragingly, and his golden beard shone brightly in the subdued morning lights. He was a brave picture at all times, so smiling and handsome, and tall, and big, with the clearest blue eyes I have ever seen and the most winning of gestures.

I was straining to watch the last of him, forcing my passage through skirts and trousers, like an excited mouse, when a lady caught me up in her arms and held me while I frantically shook my handkerchief, and he to the last stood on the wharf, kissing his hand and waving his hat to me, as if I were a grown-up person. I was enchanted with his gallant air and fine courtesy, and flung him kisses with both hands. Then I buried my head in the lady's fur, and sobbed as if my heart would break.

Ireland was receding from me, the ship was rocking, there was a sullen deafening roar of steam, and I could no longer discern the one familiar figure I gazed for in the dim indistinguishable crowd on the thin, dark shoreline. The only world I knew was fading fast before my wet glance, and in terror of another I clasped the strange lady's neck, and shivered into her soothing furs.

Chapter XIII. AT LYSTERBY.

A born traveller, the vagabond's instinct of forming pleasant friendships along the highroads that are buried with the last hand-shake showed itself on this my first voyage, and has never forsaken me throughout an accidented and varied career. I might have treasured sheaves of visiting-cards with names in every language bearing addresses in every possible town of Europe and Asia and numbers of American States. On this occasion no names or cards were exchanged between me and the lady with the sealskin coat. But she adopted me for the hours that passed until we reached Crewe, when I was ejected from the warm home of her lap, and cast out into the cold of a winter's night.

She led me by the hand to look again at the ropes and the sailors, and tumble down and scramble up the companion-stairs, while Sister Clare groaned and prayed in her cabin. Indeed, I may say that I had forgotten all about my veiled jailor, and, my tears once dried, prattled delightedly to this pretty sympathetic creature, whose lovely furs and wide hat of black plumes and black velvet made of her a princess of fairyland. Then when the caprices of the sea distressed us in our wanderings, I fell asleep in her lap, luxurious and happy, being quite at rest now about the sharks, since my new friend had patiently assured me there was nothing to fear from them.

I can now imagine what a quaint picture this motherly young lady, with the softly folding arms and the humid dusky glance, that was in itself the sweetest of caresses, may have made afterwards of our friendship, the tenderness with which she would sketch my portrait and repeat my childish confidences, the pity and indignation with which my forlornness must have filled her. A child with a home, a mother, a family, cast adrift on a grey winter's sea! Travelling from one land to another, like a valueless packet given in charge to a stranger!

I hardly remember our parting. It was late, and I was dreaming, heaven knows of what,—of the chocolate drops she had given me, or of the dear little trays of apples Bessy the applewoman sold down at Kildare. Hard arms securely caught me, and whisked me out of my delicious nest. Instead of warm fur against my cheek, I felt a blast of black-grey air, and with a howl of dismay I found myself blinking in the noisy glitter of a big station. The lady bent her charming head out of the window, smiling sadly at me from under the heavy shadow of her velvet plumed hat. I felt that she parted from me reluctantly, and knew that she had given me a passing shelter in her kind heart.

The night outside seemed bitterly cold without her protecting tenderness, and I made a stoic effort to swallow my tears, and let myself be dragged ferociously by Sister Clare, for whom I was merely baggage, to the Birmingham train. As for impressions, these were stationary, not going beyond the voice and furs of my new friend, and I was far too sorry and sleepy and weary to note anything fresh.

Lysterby, I have since been informed, is an ugly little town; but in those remote, uncritical days it appeared to me the centre of loveliness. Flowers are rare in Ireland, and here roses, red and white, grew wild and luxuriant along the lanes. But to an imaginative and romantic child, a place so peopled with legend and gay and tragic historical figures could not fail to be beautiful. In one of the common streets you looked up and saw the painted bust of a medieval knave, craning his ruffianly neck out of a window-frame, and the fellow, you were told, answered to the name of Peeping Tom. Instantly the street ceased to be real, and you were pitched pell-mell into the heart of romance.

I have not seen the place since childhood; but it remains in memory blotted, fragmentary, picturesque, an old-fashioned little town, with spired churches, rough, clean little streets, rare passers-by, never so hurried that the double file from the Ivies, under the guard of the austere ladies of Mercy, did not attract their attention, and sometimes with discomposing emphasis, as when the little street blackguards would shout after us:—

"Catholics, Catholics, quack, quack, quack, Go to the devil and never come back!"

I remember the Craven Arms, a medieval inn all hung with roses and ivy, where my parents stayed when they came to see me, and where my sister and I slept in a long low-beamed chamber, with windows made of a surprising pattern of tiny diamond squares and green lattices that excited our enthusiastic admiration. I remember the bowling-green, that appeared to roll like a sea straight to the sky, and the long, long roads with fields on either side, and the great historic ruin that has given its name to one of Scott's novels.

To me it is impossible to recall the leafy lanes, rose-scented;

the narrow pavements and sleepy little shops; the great pageant, when the town's legend became for thrilled infants an afternoon of fugitive and barbaric splendour,—without evoking vague scenes from history, and marshalling before the mind's eye brilliant and memorable figures. Dull enough, I have no doubt, for those outside the convent walls, who had to live its dull life: no discord between the outlying farmsteads and the scarcely competitive shops; the time of day not too eagerly noted, in spite of the fame of its watches; and the vociferations of the newsvendors a thing unknown. But sectarian spirit ran pretty high, if I remember rightly, and Lysterby was represented in Parliament by a fierce anti-Catholic, whose dream, we imagined, it was to hang all Jesuits and deport the nuns. His name was whispered within the convent walls in awed undertones, as a pagan persecutor may have been spoken of in the Catacombs by the early Christians. But except the veiled ladies, romantically conscious of the proximity of persecution, with the joy of a name to pronounce in shuddering alarm, all Lysterby was at peace, and free to go to bed with the lambs, with nothing to disturb it in its morning dreams less melodious than the lark's song. Private wars were of the usual anodyne and eternal character: Smith the baker not on speaking terms with Jones the butcher; Grubb the weaver, in embittered monotony of conviction, supported on unlimited quantities of beer, ready to assert every evening that Collins the miller, who lived on the other side of the common, was a scoundrel.

Of the troubles outside we little ones had no time to think. Our troubles within were abundant and absorbing, and no less absorbing and abundant were our small joys. There were ten of us only—ten queer, curious little girls; and one ragged specimen of the trousered sex—a horrid small boy, the scion of a distinguished house, whom the ladies of Mercy kept, long past the time, quaintly apparelled in black frocks and white pinafores, as an injudicious concession to claustral modesty. A boy of eight in skirts, with long brown curls upon his shoulders!

To suit his raiment, nature made him the greatest little coward and minx of the lot of us. Beside him I felt myself a brave, a gentleman, a hero of adventure. He had all the vices I intuitively abhorred. He was spiteful, a tell-tale, an ignoble whiner; and before I was a month at the Ivies I was for him "that nasty little Irish girl," whose fine furies terrified the wits out of his mean little body, whose frank boxes on a rascally small ear sent him into floods of tears, and whose masterly system of open persecution kept him ever in alarm, ever on the race to Sister This or Mother That. How we loathed that boy Frank!

On the other hand, I was speedily as popular as a creature of legend—not by reason of my virtues, which, by a rare modesty, kept themselves concealed, but because of my high spirits, untamable once let loose; my imagination, which incessantly devised fresh shudders for these timid and unimaginative children; my prodigality in invention, and my general insubordination.

The cowed and suffering baby of Ireland on Saxon shores at once revealed the Irish rebel, the instinctive enemy of law and order. I was commander-in-chief in revolt, with a most surprising gift of the gab; a satanic impulse to hurl my small weak self against authority on all occasions, and an abnormal capacity for flying out at every one with power to do me harm. Whatever may be said of the value of my courage, its quality even I the owner (who should be the last to recognise it!), must admit to be admirable. Alas! it was a virtue ever persistently wasted then as now. While it never procured me a single stroke of happiness or fortune, it has boundlessly added to the miseries of an imprudent career.

The start in Lysterby ends my patient martyrdom. Here I became the active and abominable little fiend unkindness and ill-management made of one of the gentlest and most sensitive of natures. The farther I travelled the road of childhood the more settled became my conviction that grown-up humanity, which I gradually began to loath more than even I once had feared, was my general implacable enemy. I might have grown sly and slavish in this conviction; but I am glad to say that I took the opposite course. I may be said to have planted myself against a moral wall and furiously defied all the authorities of Church and State "to come on," hitting in blind recklessness out at every one, quite indifferent to blow and defeat.

Little Angela of Kildare and Dublin, over whose sorrows I have invited the sympathetic reader to weep, was a pallid and pathetic figure. But Angela of Lysterby held her own—more even than her own, for she fought for others as well as for herself, and gave back (with a great deal more trouble at least) as much pain and affliction as she endured.

Chapter XIV. THE WHITE LADY OF LYSTERBY.

Do the ladies of Lysterby continue to train atrociously and mismanage children, to starve and thwart them, as they did in those far-off days, so remote that on looking back it seems to me now that somebody else and not I, a pacific and indifferent woman, content with most things round about me, lived those five years of perpetual passion and frantic unhappiness? Or has the old convent vanished, and carried off its long tale of incompetence, ignorance, cruel stupidity, and futile vexation?

For the seeds of many an illness were stored up in young bodies by systematic under-feeding, and hunger turned most of us into wistful little gluttons, gazing longingly into the cake-shops as we marched two by two through the tiny city, dreaming at night of Barmecide feasts, and envying the fate of the happier children at home, who devoured all the sweet things we with our empty little stomachs so bitterly remembered.

Sweet things only! Enough of bread-and-butter would have satisfied our craving. When one of us sickened and rejected the single thin slice of bread-and-butter allowed the children at breakfast, oh, the prayer and expectation of each pair of hungry eyes fixed upon the sufferer, to see to whom she would offer her neglected slice! The slice was cut in two, and usually offered, while the nun was not looking, to the children on either side. This miscarriage of appetite, we noted with regret, more frequently happened at the two tables of the big girls, where such windfalls were constantly amplifying the meagre breakfasts of somebody or other in long skirts. But we were only ten, and our appetite was pretty steady and never satisfied. Now it taxes all my heroism to visit the dentist; but then I knew each visit was a prospective joy, for, if I did not cry, the lay-teacher who conducted me thither always allowed me to buy a jam-tart, which I ate as slowly as possible in the confectioner's shop, noting the ravages of my teeth in the cake of delight with melancholy and dismay. I so loved the recompense that I used to watch anxiously for the first sign of a shaky tooth, and the instant it was removed, I was sure to shriek out excitedly—

"You see, Miss Lawson, I didn't cry a bit."

But I would not have it thought that those early school-days were days of untempered bitterness and constant ache. We were a merry lot of little savages as far as the authorities permitted us to enjoy ourselves, and life continually revealed its quaint surprises and thrilling terrors. I learnt to read with amazing rapidity, and my favourite books were of a kind liberally supplied by the convent library—Tyburn, wonderful tales of the escapes and underground adventures of Jesuits, double walls, spring-doors, mysterious passages, whitened bones in long-forgotten boxes. Thanks to my ingenuity and vivid imagination, our days became for us all a wild romance. Relegated to the infirmary by prolonged illnesses, the result of semi-starvation, naturally I had leisure to read laboriously various volumes of this edifying literature.

The infirmary itself was a chamber of legend. It was a kind of out-building to which led a long corridor behind just the sort of door my mind was fixed upon, a mere panel that in no way differed from the rest of the wainscoted wall, the very door for a Jesuit to vanish through from the pursuit of mailed myrmidons. At the end of the corridor you went down a flight of stairs, then up another flight into a pretty little green-and-white room, low beamed, with cozy cots, and long windows looking out beyond the rose-bushes, and a slip of velvet lawn, where a terrible-looking and most enchanting alley, with the trees meeting overhead, seemed to lead straight into the twilight of ghostland.

It did not take me long to see a white lady slip down that alley, like a white mist swallowed up in sombre night. No power on earth could have convinced me that I had not seen a ghost, and I stood at the window straining my eyes out in waiting for the white lady's return, with both hands frantically clasped upon my heart, which beat as if it projected a spring through my throat. White-faced and appalled, I hurried to the infirmarian, who brought me in something hot to take, and screamed out, "Oh, I've seen her, I've seen her! she was all in white, a real ghost!"

That night I was in full fever, and my poor silly little story-books were taken away. But they had done their work, and by the time I was well again my imagination had wrought out the stupendous fiction that was to communicate its thrill even to some of the big girls, and send a dozen of little girls crawling upon their knees and hands, victims of my imagination. The white lady I conceived to be the ghost of a beautiful Catholic persecuted in the days of Tyburn. She lived in this old manor-house, for we knew that the Ivies had been a manor. In her terror she had flown through the panel-door leading to the infirmary. The flight of stairs, of course, in those days continued beyond the floor, and the subterranean passage probably led round by the courtyard to the gate at the end of the dark alley. I decided that there must be several whitened bones under the floor of this corridor and the infirmary, and so convinced all my companions, even Frank, that whining little cad whom we all so heartily detested, that on play-days, during the holidays, on Sunday afternoons, every moment we could spend in secrecy, in turn two of us (companionship was necessary to add to the excitement of labour and the terrors of consequences) would crawl away from the rest with penknives and pencils, and assiduously cut away at the wooden floor until we had made a hole large enough to insert our little fists underneath. It must be admitted we always found something hard and white, which proved my theory, and those bits of dry chips we handled in awe.

For some singular months we lived upon this romance, and lived in it so intensely that all else became but a dream. Dream-like we accomplished our tasks, filled our slates with figures, copied headlines, recited verses, the dates of English history, wrought our samplers, and answered the responses of the rosary. But our thoughts, ourselves, were elsewhere, with the next beam to make a hole in, and the assurance I had given them that I had seen through a chink of the infirmary floor a white hand like marble. I was the first victim of my own invention, for I honestly believed all I said. I will not say that vanity was an alien factor in the unconscious invention. I enjoyed my power, my triumph, the fear I had inspired and so thrillingly shared—above all, I enjoyed the popularity it gave me as leader of a band of miscreants.

I do not remember how or why the fever abated. Were we found out and punished for mutilated planks? We so exaggerated the mystery of our conspiracy that it would be strange indeed if it were not discovered. But the end of the romance is completely effaced from memory. It has left no impression whatever. I see myself in turn frozen and fevered with terror, digging at every mortal spot of the convent open to the depredations of my penknife, in a wild hunt for bones and secret passages and forbidden stairs. I see the whole school enthralled by my ardent whim. And that is all.

Chapter XV. AN EXILE IN REVOLT.

What surprises me most when I recall those days is my own rapid development. The tiny inarticulate pensive creature of Ireland is, as if by magic, turned into a turbulent adventurer, quick with initiation, with a ready and violent word for my enemies, whom I regarded as many, with a force of character that compelled children older than myself to follow me; imperious, passionate, and reckless. How did it come about? It needed long months of unhappiness at home to make me revolt against the most drastic rule, and here it sufficed that a nun should doubt my word to turn me into a glorified outlaw.

I confess that whatever the deficiences of my home training, I had not been brought up to think that anybody lied. My mother never seemed to think it possible that any of her children could lie. In fact, lying was the last vice of childhood I was acquainted with. You told the truth as you breathed, without thinking of it, for the simple reason that it could not possibly occur to you not to tell the truth. This was, I knew, how I took it, though I did not reason so. I believe it was that villain Frank who broke a statue of an angel, and behind my back asserted that he had seen me do it. I had no objection in the world to break forty statues if it came in the day's work, and so far from concealing my misdeeds, I was safe to glory in any iniquity I could accomplish. So when charged with the broken angel, I said, saucily enough I have no doubt—oh! I have no wish to make light of the provocations of my enemies—that I hadn't done it.

The Grand Inquisitor was a lovely slim young nun, with a dainty gipsy face, all brown and golden, full-cheeked, pink-lipped, black-browed. I see her still, the exquisite monster, with her long slim fingers, as delicate as ivory, and the perfidious witchery of her radiant dark smile.

"You mustn't tell lies, Angela. You were seen to break the statue."

I stood up in vehement protest, words poured from me in a flood; they gushed from me like life-blood flowing from my heart, and in my passion I flung my books on the floor, and vowed I would never eat again, but that I'd die first, to make them all feel miserable because they had murdered me. And then the pretty Inquisitor carried me off, dragging me after her with that veiled brutality of gesture that marks your refined tyrant. I was locked up in the old community-room, then reserved for guests, a big white chamber, with a good deal of heavy furniture in it.

"You'll stay here, Angela, until I come to let you out," she hissed at me.

I heard the key turn in the lock, and my heart was full of savage hate. I sat and brooded long on the vengeance I desired to wreak. Sister Esmeralda had said she would come at her good will to let me out. "Very well," thought I, wickedly; "when she comes she'll not find it so easy to get in."

My desire was to thwart her in her design to free me when she had a mind to. My object was to die of hunger alone and forsaken in that big white chamber, and so bring remorse and shame upon my tyrants. So, with laboured breath and slow impassioned movements, I dragged over to the door all the furniture I could move. In my ardour I accomplished feats I could never have aspired to in saner moments. A frail child of eight, I nevertheless wheeled arm-chairs, a sofa, a heavy writing-table, every seat except a small stool, and even a cupboard, and these I massed carefully at the door as an obstruction against the entrance of my enemy.

And then I sat down on the stool in the middle of the chamber, and tore into shreds with hands and teeth a new holland overall. Evening began to fall, and the light was dim. My passion had exhausted itself, and I was hungry and tired and miserable. Had any one else except Sister Esmeralda come to the door, I should have behaved differently, for I was a most manageable little creature when not under the influence of the terrible exasperation injustice always provoked in me. But there she stood, after the repeated efforts of the gardener called up to force open my prison door, haughty, contemptuous, and triumphant, with me, poor miserable little me, surrounded by the shreddings of my holland pinafore, in her ruthless power.

A blur of light, the anger of madness, the dreadful tense sensation of my helplessness, and before I knew what I had done I had caught up the stool and wildly hurled it at her triumphant visage. Oh, how I hated Sister Esmeralda! how I hated her!

The moment was one of exceptional solemnity. I was not scolded, or slapped, or roughly treated. My crime was too appalling for such habitual treatment. One would think I already wore the black shroud of death, that the gallows stood in front of me, and beside it the coffin and the yawning grave, as my enemy, holding my feeble child's hand in a vice, marched me down the corridor into the dormitory, where a lay-sister was commanded to fetch my strong boots, my hat and cloak.

The children were going joyously off to supper, with here and there, I can imagine, an awed whisper in my concern, as the lay-sister took my hand in hers; and in silence by her side, in the grey twilight, I walked from the Ivies beyond the common down to the town convent, where only the mothers dwelt. I knew something dreadful was going to happen to me, and being tired of suffering and tired of my short troubled life, I hoped even then that it would prove death. I did not care. It was so long since I had thought it worth while caring!

And so I missed the lovely charm of that silent walk through the unaccustomed twilight, with quaint little shops getting ready their evening illumination, and free and happy persons walking to and fro, full of the joy of being, full of the bliss of freedom. My heart was dead to hope, my intelligence, weary from excess of excitement and pain, was dull to novelty.

In the town convent I was left awhile in aching solitude in the brown parlour, with its pious pictures and big crucifix. I strained eye and ear through the silent dusk, and was relieved when the superioress—a sort of female pontiff, whom we children saw in reverential stupefaction on scarce feast-days, when she addressed us from such heights as Moses on the mountain might have addressed a group of sparrows—with two other nuns entered. It looked like death, and already the heart within me was dead. I know so well now how I looked: white, blue-veined, blue-lipped, sullen, and indifferent.

My wickedness was past sermonising. I was simply led up-stairs to a brown cell, and here the red-cheeked lay-sister, a big brawny creature, stripped me naked. Naked, mind, though convent rules forbid the whipping of girls. I was eight, exceedingly frail and delicate. The superioress took my head tightly under her arm, and the brawny red-cheeked lay-sister scourged my back with a three-pointed whip till the blood gushed from the long stripes, and I fainted. I never uttered a groan, and I like to remember this infantine proof of my pride and resolute spirit.

Chapter XVI. MY FIRST CONFESSION.

The sequel is enfolded in mystery. Was I long unconscious? Was I long ill? Was there any voice among the alarmed nuns lifted in my favour? Or was the secret kept among the superioress, the lay-sister who thrashed me, and the doctor? As a Catholic in a strong and bigoted Protestant centre, in the pay of a Catholic community, it is not unreasonable to suppose him anxious to avoid a scandal. For outside there was the roaring lion, the terrible member for Lysterby, seeking the Catholics he might devour! That satanic creature who dreamed at night of Tyburn, and, if he could, would have proscribed every priest and nun of the realm! Picture the hue and cry in Parliament and out of it, if it were known that a baby girl had been thrashed by strong, virile hands, as with a Russian knout, with the ferocity of blood-thirsty jailers instead of the gentleness of holy women striving to inculcate precepts of virtue and Christian charity in the breast of a tiny reprobate! And ladies, too, devoted to the worship of mercy and of Mary, the maiden of sorrow, the mild mother of humanity.

I know I lay long in bed,—that my wounds, deep red open stripes, were dressed into scars by lint and sweet oil and herbs. The doctor, a cheery fellow with a Scottish name, came and sat by my bedside, and gave me almond-drops, and begged me repeatedly "to look up." The pavement outside was rough, the little city street was narrow, and the flies rumbling past from the station to the Craven Arms shook my bed. The noise was novel, and excited me. I thought of my imaginary friend of the Ivies, the white lady, and wondered if any one had ever thrashed her. The cook, Sister Joseph, from time to time stole up-stairs and offered me, by way of consolation, maybe a bribe, a Shrewsbury biscuit, a jam-tart, a piece of seed-cake.

Once the pain of my lacerated back subsided I was not at all bored. It was good to lie in a fresh white bed and listen dreamily to the discreet murmurs of a provincial town in the quiet convent-house, have nothing to do, no scrapes to get into, hear no scolding voices, and have plenty of nice things to eat, after the long famine of nine interminable months.

I do not remember when it was she first came to me. She was a slim, oldish nun, with a white delicate visage and eyes full of a wistful sadness, neither blue nor grey. Her voice was very low, and gave me the same intense pleasure with which the soft touch of her thin small hands thrilled me. She was called Mother Aloysius, and painted pictures for the chapel and for the convent. Did she know what had happened, and had she taken the community's debt to me upon her lean shoulders? Or was I merely for her a sick and naughty little girl, to whom she was drawn by sympathy?

She never spoke of my whipping, nor did I. Perhaps with the unconscious delicacy of sensitive childhood I divined that it would pain her. More probably still, I was only too glad to be enfolded in the mild warmth of her unquestioning tenderness. Wickedness dropped from me as a wearisome garment, and, divested of its weight, I trotted after her heels like a little lapdog. She took me with her everywhere; into the big garden where she tended the flowers, and where she allowed me to water and dig myself out of breath, fondly persuaded that the fate of the flowers next year depended upon my exertions; to her work-room, where in awed admiration I watched her paint, and held her brushes and colours for her; to the chapel where she changed the flowers, and where I gathered the stalks into little hills and swept them into my pinafore. And all the time I talked, ceaselessly, volubly,—not of past sufferings, nor of present pain, but of the things that surprised and perplexed me, of the countless things I wanted to do, of the tales of Tyburn and the white lady.

When I was well enough to go back to daily woe and insufficient food, I was dressed in hat and jacket and strong boots, and while I stood in the hall the awful superioress issued from the community-room and looked at me coldly.

"You have had your lesson, Angela. You will be a good child in future, I hope," she said, and touched my shoulder with a lifeless gesture.

The mischievous impulse of saucy speech and wicked glance died when I encountered the gentle prayer of my new friend's faded eyes. I was only a baby, but I understood as well as if I had been a hundred what those kind and troubled eyes said, glancing at me behind the woman she must have known I hated. "Be good, dear child; be silent, be respectful. Forgive, forget, for my sake." I swallowed the angry words I longed to utter on the top of a sob, and went and held up my cheek to Mother Aloysius.

"You're a brave little girl, Angela," she said, softly. "You'll see, if you are good, that reverend mother will let you come down and spend a nice long day with me soon again; and I'll take you to water the flowers and fill the vases in the chapel, and watch me paint up-stairs. Good-bye."

She kissed me on both cheeks, not in the fleshless kiss of the nun, but with dear human warmth of lips, and her fingers lingered tenderly about my head. Did she suspect the sacrifice I had made to her kindness?—the fierce and wrathful words I had projected to hurl at the head of the superioress, and that I had kept back to please her?

At the Ivies I maintained a steadfast silence upon what had happened. I cannot now trace the obscure reasons of my silence, which must have pleased the nuns, for nobody ever knew about my severe whipping. Thanks to the beneficent influences of my new friend, I was for a while a model of all the virtues. I studied hard, absorbed pages of useful knowledge in the "Child's Guide," and mastered the abstruse contents of Cardinal Wiseman's "History of England." At the end of a month, to the amazement of everybody and to my own dismay, I was rewarded with a medal of good conduct, and formally enrolled in that virtuous body, the Children of the Angels, and wore a medal attached to a brilliant green ribbon.

This transient period of grace, felt no doubt by all around me to be precarious and unstable, was deemed the fitting moment for my first confession. What a baby of eight can have to confess I know not. The value of such an institution for the infantine conscience escapes me. But there can be no question of its enormous sensational interest for us all. Two new children had made their appearance since my tempestuous arrival. They belonged to the band, as well as an idiot girl two years older than I, and now deemed wise enough to crave pardon for sins she could not possibly commit. We carefully studied the "Examination of Conscience," and spelt out the particularly big words with a thrill: they looked nice mysterious sins, the sort of crimes we felt we would gladly commit if we had the chance.

I went about sombre and dejected, under the conviction that I must have sinned the sin against the Holy Ghost, and Polly Evans wondered if adultery figured upon the list of her misdoings. She was sure, however, that she had not defrauded the labourer of his daily wage, whatever that might be, for the simple reason that she had never met a labourer. I was tortured with a fresh sensational doubt. My foster-mother's cousin at Kildare was a very nice labourer who often had given me sweets. Could I, in a moment of temporary aberration, have defrauded him of his wage? And then adultery! If Polly was sure she had committed adultery, might I not also have so deeply offended against heaven? I had not precisely killed anybody, but had I not desired to kill Sister Esmeralda the day I threw the stool at her?

And so we travelled conscientiously, like humble, but, in the very secret depths of our being, self-admiring pilgrims, over the weary and profitless road of self-examination, and assured ourselves with a fervent thrill that we were indeed miserable sinners. "I'll never get into a passion again," I swore to Polly Evans, like a monstrous little Puritan, and before an hour had passed was thirsting for the blood of some offender.

I even went so far as to include Sister Esmeralda and Frank in my offer of general amnesty to humanity; and indited at some nun's suggestion a queer epistle to my mother, something in the tone the prodigal son from afar might have used writing to his father when he first decided to abandon the husks and swine, etc. I boldly announced my intention of forsaking the path of wickedness, with a humble confession of hitherto having achieved supremacy in that nefarious kingdom, and of walking henceforth with the saints.

I added a practical postscript, that I was always very hungry, and stated with charming candour that I did not like any of the nuns except Mother Aloysius, which was rather a modification of the exuberant burst of virtue expressed on the first page. This postscript was judiciously altered past recognition, and I was ordered to copy it out: "I am very happy at Lysterby. All the dear nuns are so kind to me. We shall have a little feast soon. Please, dear mamma, send me some money."

If the money ever came, it was naturally confiscated by the dear nuns. It was not money we mites needed, but bread-and-butter and a cup of good milk, or a plate of simple sustaining porridge. However, for the moment the excitement of confession sustained us. Having communicated to each other the solemn impression that we had broken all the Commandments, committed the seven deadly sins, and made mockery of the four cardinal virtues, the next thing to decide was to what length of repentance we were bound to go. Polly Evans' enthusiasm was so exalted that she yearned to follow the example of the German emperor we had read of who walked, or crawled on his knees, I forget which, to Rome, and made a public confession to the Pope. But this we felt to be an immodest flight of fancy in a little girl who had done nothing worth speaking of. She was like my Kildare companion Mary Jane, who constantly saw herself in a personal scuffle with Queen Victoria.

When the great day came we were bidden to stay in the chapel after the rest, and then were taken down to the town convent, with instructions to keep our minds fixed upon the awful sacrament of confession as we walked two and two through the streets.

"Remember, children," said that infamous Sister Esmeralda, prettier than ever, as she fixed me with a deadly glance, "to tell a lie in the confessional box is to tell a lie to the Holy Ghost. You may be struck dead for it."

Did she mean that for me? Oh, why had I so rashly vowed myself to a life of virtue? Why had I so precipitously chosen the companionship and example of the saints? Why had I read the lives of St. Louis of Gonzaga, St. Stanislaus of Kotska, and other lamb-like creatures, and in a fit of admiration sworn to resemble them?—since all these good resolutions debarred me from flinging another stool at that lovely hostile visage. But having elected momentarily to play the part of a shocking little prig, I swallowed my wrath, with a compunctious sensation, and felt a glow all over to think I was already so much of a saint.

In the convent chapel, with our throbbing hearts in our mouths, we knelt, a diminutive row, in our Sunday uniform (I have worn so many convent uniforms that I am rather mixed about them, and cannot remember which was blue on Sunday and which was black, but the Lysterby Sunday uniform I know was black). Polly Evans was the first to disappear, swallowed up in the awful box. She issued forth, tremulous and wide-eyed, and I followed her, pallid and quaking. The square grating was closed, and the green curtain enfolded me in a terrific dusk. I felt sick and cold with fright. What was going to happen? Could something spring suddenly out and clutch me? Was the devil behind me? Had my guardian angel forsaken me? I had read a great deal of late about "a yawning abyss," "a black pit," a "bottomless hole." Was I going to tell a lie to the Holy Ghost unknowing, and so be struck dead like, like——?

The square slid swiftly back, and I saw a dim man's profile through the grating. Had I seen Father Morris clear before me, my fears would instantly have been quelled, for he was a graceful, aristocratic, soft-voiced man, quick to captivate little children by his winning smile. But that dim formless thing behind the grating, what was it? They told me the priest in the confessional was God. The statement was not such that any childish imagination could grasp. The sickness of terror overcame me, and I, whom the rough sea of the Irish Channel had not harmed, fell down in a dreadful fit of nausea that left me prostrate for days.

Chapter XVII. THE CHRISTMAS HAMPERS.

Nobody but a hungry and excitable child, exiled from home and happiness, bereft of toys and kisses, can conceive the mad delight of receiving a Christmas hamper at school. Picture, if you can, a minute regiment with eager faces pasted against the frost-embroidered window-panes, watching a van drive up the Ivies' path, knowing that a hamper is coming for some fortunate creature—but for whom?

Outside the land is all bridal white, and the lovely snow looks like deep-piled white velvet upon the lawn, and like the most delicate lace upon the branches. We see distinctly the driver, with a big good-humoured face of the hue of cochineal under his snow-covered hat, and he nods cheerfully to his enthusiastic admirers. He would be a churl indeed to remain unmoved by our vociferous salutations, as we stamp our feet, and clap our hands, and shout with all the force of our infant lungs.

For the Christmas hamper, announced by letter from my stepfather, meant for me the unknown. But every Christmas afterwards I was wiser, and not for that less glad. A hamper meant a turkey, a goose, a large plum-cake with Angela in beautiful pink letters upon the snow-frost ground. It meant boxes of prunes, of sweets, of figs, lots of oranges and apples, hot sherry and water, hot port and water in the dormitory of a cold night, all sorts of surprising toys and picture-books. But it did not imply by any means as much of those good things (I speak of the eatables) for me as my parents fancied. The nuns generously helped themselves to the lion's share of fruit and wine and fowls.

But the cake, best joy of all, was left to us untouched, and also the sweets. The big round beauty was placed in front of me; with a huge knife, a lay-sister sliced it up, and I, with a proud, important air, sent round the plate among hungry and breathless infants, who had each one already devoured her slice with her eyes before touching it with her lips.

And at night in the dormitory, all those bright eyes and flushed little faces, as we laughed and shouted and danced, disgraceful small topers that we were, drinking my stepfather's sherry and port—drinking ourselves into rosy paradises, where children lived upon plum-cake and hot negus.

Oh, the joy of those Christmas excesses, after the

compulsory sobriety of long ascetic months! As each child received a hamper, not quite so bountifully and curiously filled as mine, for my stepfather was a typical Irishman—in the matter of hospitality, of generosity, he always erred on the right side for others, and was as popular as a prince of legend,—for a fortnight we revelled in a fairyland of toffee and turkey, of sugared cakes and plum-pudding, of crackers and sweets, and apples and oranges and bewitching toys. Like heroes refreshed, we were then able to return to the frugality of daily fare—though, alas! I fear this fugitive plenty and bliss made us early acquainted with the poet's suffering in days of misery by the remembering of happier things. This was my candid epistle, soon after Christmas, despatched to Kildare:—

"My dere Evryday Mama,—i dont like skule a bit. i cant du wat i like. i dont have enuf tu et. Nun of us have enuf tu et. We had enuf at crismas when everyboddy sent us lots of things. We were very glad i had luvly things it wos so nice but i dont like skule, its horid, theres a horid boy here. i bet him when he called me a savage. Sister Esmeralda said it first i dont like her. She teches me. tell Mary Jane to give my black dog 6 kisses. i want to go home i like yu and Louis and Mary Jane and Bessy the apel woman i want to clim tres like Johny Burke your affecshunat little girl.

Angela."

When this frank outpouring was subjected to revision, it ran:—

"My dear Foster-Mamma,—I am very happy here with the dear nuns. I hope I shall remain with them a long while. We have such fun always. We learn ever so many nice things. We love our dear mistress, Sister Esmeralda. Reverend Mother had a cold, and we all prayed so hard for her, and now she is better. I want some money for her feast-day. We are going to give her a nice present. We had a play and a tea-party. Lady Wilhelmina Osborne's little girl came over from the Abbey. I hope you are quite well. With love, your affectionate

Angela."

All our mistresses were not like Sister Esmeralda, a Spanish inquisitor in a shape of insidious charm, nor a burly brute like the lay-sister, who had so piously welted my naked back, nor a chill and frozen despot like the pallid superioress. Mother Aloysius was, of course, a far-off stained-glass vision, a superlative rapture in devotion, not suitable for daily wear,—a recompense after the prolonged austerities of virtue and self-denial, a soaring acquaintance with ecstatic admiration. But on a lower plane there were some younger nuns we found tolerable and sympathetic. There was Sister Anne, who taught us to play at snowballs, and took a ball on her nose with companionable humour in the midst of our shrieking approbation. There was Sister Ignatius, who inspired us with terpsichorean ambition by dancing a polka with one of the big girls down the long study hall, to the amiable murmur of—

"Can you dance a polka? Yes, I can. Up and down the room with a nice young man";

or upon a more imaginative flight—

"My mother said that I never should Play with the gypsies in the wood; If I did, she would say, Naughty girl to disobey."

Her great feat was, however, the Varsovienne, which she told us was a Polish dance, and that Poland was a bleak and unfortunate country on the confines of Russia. Ever afterwards I associated the sprightly Sister Ignatius with a polar bear, especially when I watched her dance the "Varsovienne," and fling her head over her shoulders in a most laughable way, just as I imagined a bear would do if he took to dancing the dance of Poland.

Mother Catherine is a less agreeable memory. I see her still, a tall gaunt woman in coif and black veil, with austere grey eyes. She used to watch us in the refectory, and whenever a greedy infant kept a rare toothsome morsel for the wind-up of a frugal meal, Mother Catherine would sweep down and confiscate the reserved luxury. "My child, you will make an act of mortification for the good of your soul." I leave you to imagine the child's dislike of her immortal soul, as the goody was carried off.

Chapter XVIII. MR. PARKER THE DANCING-MASTER.

The joy of my second year at Lysterby was Mr. Parker the dancing-master. Was he evoked from pantomime and grotesque legend by the sympathetic genius of Sister Ignatius? We were all solemnly convened, in our best shoes and frocks, to a great meeting in the big hall to make the acquaintance of our dancing-master, and learn the polite steps of society. A wizen cross-looking little creature stood at the top of the long room, and as we entered in file, all agog, and ready enough, heaven knows, to shriek for nothing, from sheer animal spirits, he bowed to us, as I suppose they bowed in the good old days of Queen Anne. For Queen Anne was his weakness. I wonder why, since she was neither the queen of grace nor of beauty.

I recall the gist of his first speech: "We are now, young ladies, about to study one of the most necessary and the most serious of arts, the art of dancing. It is the art of dancing that makes ladies and gentlemen of us all. In a ball-room the awkward, those who cannot dance, are in disgrace. Nobody minds them, nobody admires them. They have not the tone of society. They are poor creatures, who, for all society cares, might never have been born. What it behoves you, young ladies, is to acquire the tone of society from your earliest years, and it is only by a steady practice of the art of dancing that you may hope to acquire it. Practice, young ladies, makes perfect—remember that."

Ever afterwards, his first question, before beginning each week's lesson, was: "What does practice do, young ladies?" and we were all expected to reply in a single ringing voice: "Makes perfect, Mr. Parker." Children are heartless satirists, and the follies of poor little Mr. Parker filled us with wicked glee.

I see him still, unconscious tiny clown, gathering up in a delicate grasp the tails of his black coat to show us how a lady curtseyed in the remote days of Queen Anne. And mincing across the polished floor, he would say, as he daintily picked his steps: "The lady enters the ball-room on the tip of her toes—so!" Picture, I pray you, the comic appearance of any woman who dared to enter a ball-room as Mr. Parker walked across our dancing-hall! Society would stand still to gape. He minced to right, he minced to left, he minced in and out of the five positions, and then with eyes ecstatically closed, he would seize his violin, and play the homely air of "Nora Creina," as he *chasséed* up and down the floor for our delectation, singing the while—

"Bend and rise-a—Nora Creina, Rise on your toes-a—Nora Creina, Chassez to the right-a—Nora Creina, And then to the left-a—Nora Creina."

In his least inspired moments, he addressed us in the first position; but whenever he soared aloft on the wings of imagination, he stood in the glory of the fifth. In that position he never failed to recite to us the imposing tale of his successes in the "reception halls" of the Duchess of Leamington and the Marchioness of Stoke. Once he went so far as to exhibit to us a new dance he had composed expressly for his illustrious friend the duchess.

"My dears, that dance will be all the rage next spring in London, you will see."

He was quite aware that we never would see, having nothing on earth to do with the London season. But the assertion mystified us, and enchanted him.

"Thus my hand lightly reposes on the waist of her Grace, her fingers just touch my shoulders, and, one, two, three—boom!" he was gliding round the room, clasping lightly an imaginary duchess in his arms, in beatific unconsciousness of the exquisite absurdity of his appearance and action, and we children followed his circumvolutions with glances magnified and brightened by mirth and wonderment.

The irresistible Mr. Parker had a knavish trick of keeping us on our good behaviour by a delusive promise persistently unfulfilled. Every Tuesday, after saluting us in the fashion of the eighteenth century and demanding from us an immense simultaneous curtsey of Queen Anne, holding our skirts in an extravagant semicircle and trailing our little bent bodies backward and upward upon the most pointed of toes, he would rap the table with his bow, clear his throat, adjust his white tie, straighten himself, and, with a hideous grin he doubtless deemed captivating, he would address us inclusively—

"Young ladies, it is my intention to bring you a little confectionery next Tuesday; and now, if you please, attention! and answer. What does practice do?"

In vain we shouted our customary response with more than our customary conviction; the confectionery was always for next Tuesday, and never, alas! for to-day. With longing eyes we watched the slightest movement of the master towards his pocket. He never produced anything but his handkerchief, and when he doubled in two to wish us "O reevoyer," he never omitted to say—

"To-day I did not pass by the confectioner's shop; but it will certainly be for next Tuesday."

For a long time he took us in, as other so-called magicians have taken in simpletons as great as we. We believed he had a secret understanding with the devil, for only to the power of evil could we attribute a quickness of apprehension such as he boasted. He would stand with his back to us, playing away at his violin, while we *chasséed* and *croiséd* and heaven knows what else—

"Now, my senses are so acutely alive to the impropriety of a false step, young ladies, that even with my back turned to you, I shall be able to tell which of you has erred without seeing her."

Sure enough he always pounced on the bungler, and never failed to switch round his bow violently and hit her toes. How was it done? Simply enough, one of us discovered quite by accident. There was a big mahogany press, as finely polished as a mirror, and in front of this the master planted himself. The rows of dancers, from crown to heel, were as clear to him as in a glass. By such simple means may a terrible reputation be acquired. For months had Mr. Parker shabbily usurped the fame of a magician.

In his quality of master he could permit himself a brutality of candour not usually shown by his sex to us without the strictest limits of intimacy. There was a big girl of sixteen, very stout, very tall, squarely built, with poultry-yard writ in broad letters over her whole dull and earthly form. An excellent creature, I have no doubt, though I knew nothing whatever about her, being half her age, which in school constitutes a difference of something approaching half a century. Her name was Janet Twycross, and she came from Shakespeare's town. As befits a master of the graceful art, Mr. Parker's preference was, given to the slim and lovely nymph, and such a square emblem of the soil as Janet Twycross would naturally provoke his impatient contempt. Possibly she merited all the vicious rage he showered on her poor big feet, pathetically evident, emerging from skirts that just reached her ankles. But with my larger experience and knowledge of his sex, I am inclined to doubt it, and attribute his vindictiveness to a mere masculine hatred of ugliness in woman rather than to the teacher's legitimate wrath. Hardly a Tuesday went by but he sent the inoffensive, great, meek creature into floods of tears; and while she wept and sobbed, looking less lovely than ever in her sorrow, he would snarl and snicker at her, imitate her jeeringly, and cast obloquy on her unshapely feet.

"A ploughboy would be disgraced by such feet as Miss Twycross's," he would hiss across at her, and then rap them wickedly with his bow.

The art of dancing, Mr. Parker proved to us, is insufficient to make a gentleman of its adept. Once his unsleeping fury against the unhappy girl carried him to singular lengths. He bade us all be seated, and then, with his customary inflated and foolish air began to address us upon the power of art. With art you can achieve anything, you can even lend grace to the ungraceful.

"I will now chose from your ranks the most awkward, the most pitiable and clumsy of her sex. The young lady unassisted cannot dance a single step; but such is my consummate skill, so finished is my art, that I shall actually succeed in bestowing some of my own grace as a dancer upon her. Advance, Miss Twycross."

I leave you to picture the sensations of the unfortunate so addressed and so described. She advanced slowly, square and sodden, but with an unmistakable look of anguish in her poor harassed eyes, of a blue as dull and troubled as her complexion; and a certain twitching of her thin tight lips was eloquent enough of her unprovoked hurt.

Mr. Parker, with his simpering disgusted air of ill-natured little dandy, flourished a perfumed handkerchief about her face, to sustain his affronted nerves, no doubt, placed an arm gingerly about the flat square waist, clasped her outer hand in evident revulsion, and began to scamper and drag her round the room in the steps of a wild schottische. Most of us tittered—could we be expected to measure the misery of the girl, while nature made us excruciatingly alive to the absurdity of her tormentor?

As a girl myself I have often laughed in recalling the incident; but I own that the brute should have been kicked out of the establishment for such an object-lesson in the art of communicating grace. As for his boasted achievement, even we babies could perfectly understand that there was not much to choose between his jerky waxwork steps and the heavy stamp of his partner. She at least was true to nature and moved as she looked, an honest cow-like creature, whom you were at liberty not to admire, but who offered you no reason to despise her. While he, her vindictive enemy, mean unnatural little body, sheathing a base, affected, silly little soul, fiddling and scraping away his days which were neither dignified nor manly, he offered himself to the unlimited contempt of even such microscopic humanity as ours. We felt he was not a man with the large capacity of manhood, but a disgraced and laughable thing, a puppet moving upon springs and speaking artificially, manufactured as dolls are, for the delectation of little folk.

We enjoyed Mr. Parker, but we never regarded him as more human than the clown or the harlequin of the pantomime. We imitated him together; we played *at him*, as we played at soldiers or fairies or social entertainment. Had we learnt that he was dead or ill, or driven to the poorhouse, it would have been just as if we had heard such news of harlequin, or heard that Peeping Tom had fallen from his window and smashed his head. Mr. Parker was not a person at the Ivies; he was a capital joke.

Chapter XIX. EPISCOPAL PROTECTION.

The succeeding years in Lysterby are obscured. Here and there I recall a vivid episode, an abiding impression. Papa came over with one of my elder sisters. They arrived at night, and I, half asleep, was dressed hurriedly and taken down to the parlour. A big warm wave of delight overwhelmed me as my stepfather caught me in his arms and whisked me up above his fair head. It was heaven to meet his affectionate blue eyes dancing so blithely to the joy of my own. Seated upon his shoulder, I touched a mole on his broad forehead, and cried, as if I had made a discovery—

"You've got the same little ball on your forehead, papa, that you had when you used to come down to Kildare."

Bidding me good-night, he promised to come for me early next day, and told me I should sleep in the Craven Arms, and spend two whole days driving about the country with him. How comforting the well-filled table, the cold ham, the bacon and eggs at breakfast, the bread and marmalade, all served on a spotless tablecloth, and outside the smell of the roses and honeysuckle, and the exciting rumble of flies up and down the narrow street! I was so happy that I quite forgot my woes, and did not remember to complain of my enemies. There was so much to eat, to see, to think of, to feel, to say! I not only wanted to know all about everybody at home, but I wanted to see and understand all about me.

In the Abbey we saw Vandyke's melancholy Charles, and it was a rare satisfaction for me to be able to tell how he had been beheaded. At the great Castle we saw Queen Elizabeth's bed with the jewel-wrought quilt, and my romantic elder sister, fresh from reading "The Last of the Barons," passionately kissed the King-maker's armour. She told us the thrilling tale as we sat in the famous cedar avenue, when the earl's daughter, all summery in white muslin and Leghorn hat, passed us with her governess, and although she was a fresh slip of a girl just like my sister, because of her name we felt that a living breath of history had brushed us. She was not for us an insignificant girl of our own century, but something belonging to the King-maker, a breathing memory of the Wars of the Roses, the sort of creature the dreadful Richard might have wooed in his hideous youth.

And then at night, in the old inn, we discovered two big illustrated volumes about Josephine and Napoleon. I had not got so far in history as Napoleon, and here was an unexplored world, whose fairy was my voluble and imaginative sister. With a touch of her wand she unrolled before my enthralled vision scenes of the French Revolution and the passionate loves of Bonaparte and the young Viscountess de Beauharnais. I wish every child I know two such nights as I passed, listening to this evocative creature revive so vividly one of the intensest and most dramatic hours of history. Thanks to her eloquence, to her genius, Napoleon, vile monster, became one of my gods. I think the thrilling tale she read me was by Miss Muloch. Impossible now to recall the incidents that sufficed to turn succeeding weeks into an exquisite dream. Who, for instance, was the beauteous creature in amber and purple velvet, with glittering diamonds, that usurped such a fantastic place in the vague aspirations of those days? And the lovely Polish countess Napoleon loved? And those letters from Egypt to Josephine, and Josephine's shawls and flowers, and the ghost-stories of Malmaison, and the last adieu the night before the divorce. Hard would it be to say whom I most loved and deeply pitied, the unadmirable Josephine or the admirable queen of Prussia. My sister read aloud, as we sat up in bed together, I holding the candle, and gazing in awe and delight, wet-eyed, at the coarse engravings.

Other sisters came in quick succession, but they remained strangers to me. They fawned on Sister Esmeralda, whom I hated: they were older and wiser than I; they aspired to the ribbon of the Children of Mary, and walked submissively with the authorities of Church and State. They played "Il Baccio" on the piano, and a mysterious duet called the "Duet in D." The only sister I remember of those days as an individual was Pauline, who had opened to me a world of treasures. At school, she naturally forsook me for girls of her own age; but on play-days, when we were free to do as we liked all day, she sometimes condescended to recall my existence, and told me with an extraordinary vivacity of recital the stories of "East Lynne," "The Black Dwarf," "Rob Roy," and "Kenilworth."

But for the rest she was a great and glorious creature who dwelt aloft, and possessed the golden key of the chambers of fiction. My immediate friend was Polly Evans, whose mamma once took me to tea in an old farmhouse along the Kenilworth road.

There were strawberries and cream on the table, and delicious little balls of butter in blue-and-white dishes, and radishes, which I had never before eaten; and the air was dense with the smell of the flowers on table, sideboard, mantelpiece, and brackets. Polly and I, with her brother Godfrey, played all the long afternoon in the hay-field, drunk with the odour, the sunny stillness, the hum of the bees—drunk, above all, with this transient bliss of freedom and high living.

Another time Mrs. Evans took me with Polly and Godfrey to Kenilworth Castle, where we dined among the ruins on ham, cold chicken, fruit, and lemonade. Yet she herself is no remembered personality: I cannot recall a single feature of hers, and even Polly herself is less clear in memory than Mary Jane of Kildare, than the abominable Frank.

Years after, Polly and her brother visited Ireland as tourists, and having all that time treasured my parents' address, called to see me. But I was abroad, a hopeless wanderer. Godfrey, I learnt, was quite a fine young fellow, who shared his sister's attachment to me. Polly was sprightly and pretty, it seems, engaged too. But I never saw them again.

An eminent bishop came to confirm us, and we were taken down to town church, where, to our infinite amusement, we occupied several rows of benches opposite a boys' school, also brought hither for the same ceremony, each with a white rosette in his button-hole. None of us took the rite very seriously. We found it droll to be tapped on the cheek by a white episcopal hand and told that we were soldiers, and we watched the boys to see if their bearing were more martial than ours. They seemed equally preoccupied with us, and looked as if they felt themselves fools, awkward and shamefaced. They stared hard at our noble youth, Frank, in his eternal skirts—his curls had recently been clipped—and nudged and giggled. Much of a soldier looked Frank! Heaven help the religion of Christ or the Constitution if either reposed faith in his prowess!

Whither has he drifted, and what has life made of the meanest little rascal I ever knew? Has he learnt to tell the truth at least? Has some public school licked him into shape, and kicked the cowardice and spitefulness out of him? When I became acquainted with Barnes Newcome afterwards, I always thought of that boy Frank. "Sister So-and-so, that nasty Angela is teasing me." "Mother This, I can't eat my bread-and-milk; that horrid Angela has put salt into it." And then, when no one was looking, and a child weaker than himself was at hand, what sly pinches, and kicks, and vicious tugs at her hair. Noble youth, future pillar of the British empire, I picture you an admirable hypocrite and bully!

I wonder why the bishop singled me out of all that small crowd for a stupendous honour. He had asked my name, and after a luxurious lunch with a few privileged mothers in the convent, he requested somebody to fetch me. The nuns did not fail to impress the full measure of this honour upon me, and when I came into the refectory, where the bishop was enthroned like a prince, I caught a reassuring beam from my dear friend, Mother Aloysius!

The bishop pushed back his chair and held out both arms to me. I was a singularly pretty child, I know. My enemy, Sister Esmeralda, had even said that I had the face of an angel with the heart of a fiend. A delicate, proud, and serious little visage, with the finish, the fairness, the transparency of a golden-haired doll, meant to take the prize in an exhibition. But this would hardly explain the extraordinary distinction conferred on me by a man who has passed into history,—a grave and noble nature, with as many cares as a Prime Minister, a man who saw men and women in daily battalions, and to whom a strange little girl of nine he had never spoken to, could scarcely seem a more serious creature in life than a rabbit or a squirrel.

He had a kind and thoughtful face, deeply lined and striking. I liked his smile at once, and went up to him without any feeling of shyness.

He lifted me on to his knee, kissed my forehead, and looked steadily and long into my steady eyes. Then he kissed me again, and called for a big slice of plum-cake, which Mother Aloysius, smiling delightedly at me, was quick to hand him. He took it from the plate, and placed it in my willing grasp.

"A fine and most promising little face," I distinctly heard him say to the superioress. "But be careful of her. A difficult and dangerous temperament, all nerves and active brain, and a fearful suffering little heart within. Manage her, manage her. I tell you there's the stuff of a great saint or a great sinner here, if she should see twenty-one, which I doubt."

Alas! I have passed twenty-one years and years ago, with difficulty, it is true, with ever the haunting shadow of death about me, and time has revealed me neither the saint nor the sinner, just a creature of ordinary frailty and our common level of virtue. If I have not exactly gone to perdition—an uncheerful proceeding my sense of humour would always guard me from—I have not scaled the heights. I have lived my life, by no means as well as I had hoped in the days we are privileged to hope and to dream, not as loftily, neither with distinction nor success; but I have not accomplished any particular villainy, or scandal, or crime that would justify my claiming an important place in the ranks of sinners. I have had a good deal more innocent fun, and known a great deal more suffering, than fall to the common lot; and I have enjoyed the fun with all the intensity of the mercurial Irish temperament, and endured the other with what I think I may proudly call the courage of my race. I have not injured or cheated a human being, though I have been greatly injured and cheated by more than I could now enumerate. There ends my scaling of the hill of virtues.

Of my sins it behoves me not to speak, lest I should fall into the grotesque and delightful attitude of the sailor I once heard in London make his public confession to a Salvation Army circle.

"My brothers, I am a miserable sinner. In Australia I murdered a man; I drank continually, I thieved, I ran after harlots, and led the life of debauchery. Oh, my friends, pray for me, for now I am converted and know Jesus. I am one of the just, may I remain so. But wicked and debauched and drunken as I was, there were lots more out there much worse than I." In summing up our errors and frailties, it is always a kindly comfort offered our conceit to think that there are on all sides of us "lots more much worse than we." Unless our pride chooses to take refuge in the opposite reflection, so we prefer to glory in being much worse than others.

And so ends my single interview with an eminent ecclesiastic. He kissed me repeatedly, and stroked my hair while I munched my plum-cake on his knee. He questioned me, and discovered my passionate interest in Napoleon and Josephine and the Queen of Prussia, the King-maker, and the children in the Tower. And then, having prophesied my early death and luminous or lurid career, he filled my two small hands with almond-drops and toffee, and sent me away, a being henceforth of something more than common clay.

From that hour my position in Lysterby was improved. I was never even slapped again, though I had had the stupendous good luck to see, unseen myself, the lay-sister who had flogged me go into a cupboard on the staircase, whose door, with the key on the outside, opened outward, and crawling along on hands and knees, reached the door in time to lock her in. I was also known to have climbed fruit-trees, when I robbed enough unripe fruit to make all the little ones ill. Yet nobody beat me, and I was let off with a sharp admonishment. I went my unruly way, secretly protected by the bishop's admiration.

If I did not amend, and loved none the more my tyrants, their rule being less drastic, I had less occasion to fly out at them. Besides, semi-starvation had subdued me for the while. I suffered continually from abscesses and earache, and spent most of my time in the infirmary, dreaming and reading.

Chapter XX. HOME FOR THE HOLIDAYS.

Home for the holidays! What a joyous sound the words have for little ears! Holidays—home! Two iridiscent words of rainbow-promise, expectation in all its warm witchery of dream and enchantment, of indolence and eager activity, of impulses unrestrained, and of constant caresses. For me, alas! how much less they meant than for happier children; but even to me the change was delightful, and I welcomed the hopes it contained with all the lively emotions of imaginative childhood. First there was the excitement of the voyage, then the fresh acquaintance with the land I had left two years ago, my own quaint and melancholy land I was about to behold again through foreign glasses; then the captivation of my importance in the family circle, the wonderful things to tell, the revelations, the surprises, embroidered fact so close upon the hidden heels of invention!

My mother came to take me home. She stayed at the Ivies. It was summer-time, and all the rose-bushes were blood-red with blossom, and one breathed the fragrance of roses as if one were living a Persian poem. Not a white rose anywhere, but red upon red, through every tone from crimson to pink. Is it an exaggeration of imagination, or were the Lysterby lanes and gardens rivers of red, like the torrent-beds of the Greek isles when the oleander is a-bloom? For, looking back to the summers of Lysterby, I see nothing on earth but roses, multiplied like the daisies of the field, a whole county waving perfumed red in memory of the great historic house whose emblem in a memorable war was the red rose of Lysterby.

Of my mother's stay at the Ivies, though she stayed there several days, I remember little definite but two characteristic scenes. Walking across the lawn toward where she stood in the sunshine talking to Sister Esmeralda, I see her still as vividly now as then. She made so superb a picture that even I, who saw her through a hostile and embittered glance, stopped and asked myself if that imperial creature really were my mother. The word mother is so close, so familiar, so everyday an image, and this magnificent woman looked as remote as a queen of legend. Her very beauty was of a nature to inspire terror, as if the mere dropping of her white gold-fringed lids meant the sentence of death to the beholder. My companions round about me were prone in abject admiration, and of their state I took note with some measure of pride.

Not so had Polly Evans's mother been regarded; not so was even Lady Wilhelmina, the Catholic peeress who came to benediction on Sunday, regarded, though she had the haughty upper lip and inscrutable gaze of sensational fiction.

How to paint her, as she stood thus valorously free to the raking sunbeams that showed out the mild white bloom and roseleaf pink of her long, full visage? She wore on her abundant fair hair a black lace bonnet, trimmed with mauve flowers and a white aigrette, and the long train of her white alpaca gown lay upon the grass like a queen's robe. I remember my admiration of the thousand little flounces, black-edged, that ran in shimmering lines up to her rounded waist. She was in half mourning for my grandmother, whose existence I had forgotten all about, and brave and becoming, it must be admitted, were those weeds of mitigated grief. As I approached, she turned her fine and finished visage, with the long delicate and cruel nostrils, and the thin delicate red lips, to me, and her cold blue glance, falling upon my anxious and distrustful face, turned my heart to stone. I felt as Amy Robsart, my favourite heroine, must have felt when she encountered the gaze of royal Elizabeth. Elizabeth, handsome, tall, and stately, with long sloping shoulders and full bust, not the Elizabeth of history; an Empress Eugenie without her feminine charm and grace, of the most wonderful fairness I have ever seen, and also the most surprising harshness of expression. I have all my life been hearing of my mother's beauty, and have heard that when the Empress Eugenie's bust was exposed at the Dublin Exhibition, the general cry was that my mother had been the sculptor's model, so singular and striking was the resemblance between these two women of Scottish blood. But then and then only, in one brief flash, did I seize the insistent claim of that beauty always closed to my hostile glance. Then and then only was I compelled, by the sheer splendour of the vision, to own that the mother who did not love me was the handsomest creature I had ever beheld.

The other episode connected with her visit that has stamped itself upon memory is typical of her rare method of imparting knowledge to the infant mind. We were driving in a fly through the rose-smelling country, and it transpired, as we approached a railway station, that we were going to visit Shakespeare's grave. "Who is Shakespeare?" I flippantly asked, looking at my sister, who sat beside my mother.

Pif-paf! a blow on the ear sent sparks flying before my eyes, and rolled my hat to the ground. Two years inhabiting a sacred county and not to have heard of the poet's name! a child of hers, the most learned of women, so ignorant and so unlettered! Thus was I made acquainted with the name of Shakespeare, and with stinging cheek and humiliated and stiffened little heart, is it surprising that I remember nothing else of that visit to his tomb? Indeed it was part of my pride to look at nothing, to note nothing, but walk about that day in full-eyed sullen silence.

My mother had not seen me for two years. This was the measure of maternal tenderness she had treasured up for me in that interval, and so royally meted out to me. Other children are kissed and cried over after a week's absence. I am stunned by an unmerited blow when I rashly open my lips after a two years' separation. And yet I preserve my belief in maternal love as a blessing that exists for others, born under a more fortunate star, though the bounty of nature did not reserve a stray beam to brighten the way for that miserable little waif I was those long, long years ago.

Chapter XXI. OLD ACQUAINTANCE.

The most vivid remembrance of my first return to Ireland is the sharp sensation of ugly sound conveyed in the flat Dublin drawl. I have never since been able to surmount this unjust antipathy to the accent of my native town. The intolerable length of the syllables, the exaggerated roundness of the vowel sounds, the weight and roll of the eternal r's—it is all like the garlic of Provence, more seizing than captivating.

And then the squalor, the mysterious ugliness of the North Wall! The air of affronted leisure that greets you on all sides. A filthy porter slouches over to you, with an indulgent, quizzical look in his kindly eyes. "Is it a porther ye'll be wanting?" he asks, in suppressed wonderment at any such unreasonable need on your part. When he has sufficiently recovered from the shock, he lounges in among the boxes, heroically resolved to make a joke of his martyrdom. He meets your irritated glance with a reassuring smile, nods, and drawls out cheerily: "Aisy, now, aisy. Sure an' 'twill be all the same in a hundred years." When at last your trunks are discovered in the disorderly heap, he volunteers, with the same suggestion of indifferent indulgence: "I suppose 'twill be a cab or a cyar you'll be wanting next." By implication you are made to understand that the cab or the cyar is another exorbitant demand on your part, and that properly speaking you should shoulder your trunk yourself and march off contentedly to your inn or lodging or palace. "If ye loike, I'll lift it on to the cab for you," he adds, good-naturedly.

There are travellers whom these odd ways of Erin amuse; others there are who are exasperated to the verge of insanity by them. But they amply explain the lamentable condition of the island and the imperturbable good-humour of the least troubled and least ambitious of races. The porter's philosophy resumes the philosophy of the land: "Aisy, now, aisy. Sure an' 'twill be all the same in a hundred years."

With patience and good-humour on your side, and much voluble sympathy and information on that of your driver, you are sure to arrive somewhere, even from such remote latitudes as that of the North Wall and the Pigeon-house. You are jerked over two lock-bridges, and you thank your stars with reason that the discoloured and malodorous waters of the Liffey have not closed over you and your luggage. The catastrophe would find your driver phlegmatic and philosophic, with a twinkle in his eye above the infamous depths of mire that suffocated you, assuring you that when a man is ass enough to travel he must take the consequences of his folly. For Erin and Iberia, moist shamrock and flaunting carnation, meet in their conviction that the sage sits at home and smokes his pipe or twangs his guitar in leisure while the fool alone courts the perils of foreign highways.

As soon as the hall-door opened, and I stood with my foot upon the first step of the familiar stairs, a chorus of young voices shouted my name in glee. "An—gel—a!"

How flat and strange and inharmonious sounded that first greeting of my name in ears attuned to accents shriller and more thin! The English Angela was quick and clear; but the long-drawn Dublin Angela set all my teeth on an edge, and such was the shock that the ardour of my satisfaction in seeing them all again, and of appearing in their midst as a travelled personage, was damped.

"How odd you all talk," I remember remarking at tea, and being promptly crushed: "It's you with your horrid English accent that talks odd."

Still, in spite of this slight skirmish, they were glad enough to see me. The quaint little booby of Kildare, whom they had bullied to their liking, had grown into a lean, delicate, and resolute fiend, prepared to meet every blow by a buffet, every injustice by passionate revolt. I no longer needed Mrs. Clement's submissive protection. I had tasted the glory of independent fight, and henceforth my tormentors were entitled to some meed of pity, though justice bids me, in recording my iniquities, to remember that their misfortunes were merited and earned with exceeding rigour.

The first thrill of home-coming, that inexplicable vibration of memory's chord, which so early marks the development of the creature, and signifies the sharp division of past and present, ran like a flame through all my body when the noise of Mrs. Clement's big bunch of keys, rattling below stairs, reached me through the open drawing-room door.

"Mrs. Clement is down-stairs!" I shouted joyously, and instantly the band of blond-headed scamps carried me off in triumph.

Into whose hands has that sombre town-house of my parents passed? Heaven grant the children that play there are happier than ever I was; but if the old store-room, with the big linen-presses, and the long china-press with upper doors of wire-screen, the long table and square mahogany and leather armchairs and sofa, gives to the occupants to-day half the pleasure it always gave me, they are not to be pitied whatever their fate.

The wide window looked out upon a hideous little street, but in front there was a stone terrace, with two huge eagles, where Mrs. Clement kept pots of plants and flowers that, alas! never bloomed, watered she them never so sedulously; and above the terraces, if you ignored the sordid street, the sunset traced all its fairest and rarest effects upon the broad arch of heaven that spanned the street opening. Those Irish skies! you must go to Italy and Greece to find hues as heavenly. How many a sorrow unsuspected, that filled me with such intensity of despair as only childhood can feel, has been smoothed by that mysterious slip of sky between two dull rows of houses, against which in the liquid summer of blue dusk the eagles, with all the lovely significance of a romantic image, were sketched in sculptured stone. I dried my eyes to dream of lands where eagles flew as common as sparrows. I cannot now tell why, but I remember well that I grew to associate that distant glimpse of heaven from the old store-room with the isle of Prospero and Miranda. And when I learnt the Sonnets—which I knew by heart, as well as "The Tempest" and "The Merchant of Venice" before the holidays were over—I always found some strange connection between the abortive, sickly cowslips and primroses Mrs. Clement cultivated on her terrace in wooden boxes and those magic lines—

"From you have I been absent in the spring, When proud-pied April, dressed in all his trim, Hath put a spirit of youth in everything."

What can it be that poetry says to children, since they can neither understand the rhythm, nor metre, nor beauty, nor sentiment of it? And the child who (as I was then) is susceptible to the charm of poetry that sweeps through the infinite, weeps with delicious emotion without the ghost of an idea why. I was but a child of nine, when my sister in response to my prayer, with my cheek still stinging from that blow along the Warwick road, opened the fairyland of Shakespeare to me. With a rapture I would I now could feel, I thrilled to the glamour of the moonlight scene of the "Merchant." We never went to bed without rehearsing it, each in turn being Jessica or Lorenzo. I only remember one other sensation as passionate and vivid and absorbing, my first hearing of the Moonlight Sonata, also at an age when it was perfectly impossible that I should understand more than a mouse or a linnet a particle of its beauty or meaning. Yet there they stand out in extraordinary relief from a confusion of childish impressions, two distinct moments of inexplicable ecstasy, the reveries of Lorenzo and Jessica and the impassioned utterance of the master's soul in the divinest of sound played, possibly not well, by my eldest sister's governess in a soft summer twilight so long ago.

Meanwhile I have left Mrs. Clement, excited and pathetic, holding my thin little visage in the cup of her folded palms. She was just as faded and fair and melancholy as ever, and the same young man's head showed in the brooch frame on the unchanged black silk gown. She kissed me several times, and stroked my hair, and expressed amazement at the change in me. And while she, dear kindly soul, was only thinking of me, there was I, volatile little rascal, looking around me, delighted to see again the beautiful big red-and-white cups, and smell the spices of the cupboard. Has tea, have bread-and-milk, ever tasted again as these modest luxuries tasted in those beautiful cups? The very remembrance of them brings the water of envy to the mouth of age. I forget the miseries of childhood only to recall the pleasure I took in that warm and rich pottery, and the brilliant effect of bowls and plates and cups upon the morning and evening damask.

And that first night at home, four little girls sleeping together in two large beds, three night-dressed forms perched on a single bed, while I, the stranger returned from abroad, mimicked Mr. Parker for their shrieking delight, and held my night-dress high up on either side to perform the famous curtsey of Queen Anne. And then a furious shout outside on the landing, and my mother's voice—

"What's the meaning of that noise? Go to sleep instantly, or I'll come in and whip you all round."

A sudden scamper of white-robed limbs, and in a twinkling four heads are hidden under the sheets. Silence down the corridors, silence throughout the high old house; only the breathing of night, and four little heads are again bobbing over the pillows.

"Oh, I say, Angela, we didn't tell you, there's a new baby up-stairs. Susanna! Did you ever hear of such a name? Everybody has pretty names but us. Birdie was so jealous when it came, because nurse said her nose would be out of joint, that she tried to smash its head with a poker one day. She was caught in time."

And so there was. Another lamentable little girl born into this improvident dolorous vale of Irish misery. Elsewhere boys are born in plenty. In Ireland,—the very wretchedest land on earth for woman, the one spot of the globe where no provision is made for her, and where parents consider themselves as exempt of all duty, of tenderness, of justice in her regard, where her lot as daughter, wife, and old maid bears no resemblance to the ideal of civilisation,—a dozen girls are born for one boy. The parents moan, and being fatalists as well as Catholics, reflect that it is the will of God, as if they were not in the least responsible; and while they assure you that they have not wherewith to fill an extra mouth, which is inevitably true, they continue to produce their twelve, fifteen, or twenty infants with alarming and incredible indifference. This is Irish virtue. The army of inefficient Irish governesses and starving illiterate Irish teachers cast upon the Continent, forces one to lament a virtue whose results are so heartless and so deplorable. If my most sympathetic and most satisfactory race were only a little less virtuous in its own restricted sense of the word, and a tiny bit more rational! And not content, alas! with the iniquity of driving these poor maimed creatures upon foreign shores in the quest of daily bread, hopelessly ill-equipped for the task, without education, or knowledge of domestic or feminine lore, incapable of handling a needle or cooking an egg, without the most rudimentary instinct of order or personal tidiness, incompetent, and vague, and careless,—these same parents at home expect these martyrs abroad to replenish their coffers with miserably earned coin. I have never met an Irish governess on the Continent who had a sou to spend on her private pleasures, for the simple reason that she sent every odd farthing home. It's the iniquitous old story. Irishmen go to America, marry, and make their fortunes; but the landlord and shopkeeper at home are paid by the savings of the peasant-girls, without a "Thank you" from their parents. Let Jack or Tom send them a five-pound note in the course of a prosperous career, "Glory be to God, but 'tis the good son he is," piously ejaculate the old folk. Let Bessy or Jane give them her heart's blood, deny herself every pleasure, not only the luxuries but the very necessaries of life, and the same old folk nod their sapient heads,—"'Tis but her duty, to be sure."

Needless to say, this inappropriate burst of indignation was not inspired in those days by the sight of my new little sister in her cradle, as white as milk, with eyes like big blue stars, the eyes of her Irish father, soft and luminous and gay. She dwelt on earth just eighteen months, and then took flight to some region where it is to be hoped she found a warmer nest than fate would have offered her here below.

My grandmother was dead, but Dennis and Mary Ann still lived with my uncle Lionel. What a joy our meeting! So "thim English" hadn't made mince-meat of me! I was whole and sound, Mary Ann remarked, but mighty spare of flesh and colour. "Just a rag of a creature," Dennis commented, as he lifted my arm. "Why didn't ye write and tell us ye were hungry, alannah?"

"I did so," I promptly retorted; "but Sister Esmeralda rubbed it out, and put in something else which wasn't a bit true."

"Troth, and 'tis meself 'ud enjoy givin' that wan a piece of me moind."

The whiff of the brogue was strong enough to waft you to the clouds. But how good to be with these two honest souls again! Uncle Lionel gave me a crown-piece, when he had tortured my check with his chaven chin, and called me a little renegade because of my English accent, and then I went out to the garden, neglected ever since the death of my grandfather.

Where was Hamlet, and whither had vanished Elsinore? Where was the youth with the future revolutionary name, who used to come bounding over the hedge, cheerily humming "Love among the Roses"? There were no roses now, and the house next door was to let.

After the trim gardens of England, this desolate old slip of garden, where weeds and thick grasses grew along the uncared paths, seemed a cemetery of dead seasons. Fruit-trees that bore neither blossom nor fruit; flower-beds where never leaf nor flower now bloomed; alleys where last year's autumn leaves still lay; broken pots that used to make such a gay parterre of geraniums of every hue when my grandfather lived; defoliaged rose-bushes, now mere summer urns of unfulfilled promise, and scarce a red bunch on the currant-boughs. And the pool, with the circle of watering-cans above, now rusty and untouched, where I used to watch for the first faint line of shadow cast by the gathering dusk, which stole across its clear face in keeping with the stealing flight of light above—how dead and sad all this seemed, despite its quaint familiarity. I was but a child, and yet as I stood once more in that neglected garden, I had some premonition of the immitigable sadness of remembrance, the feeling that there was already a past that had slipped through my fingers, as the waters run ceaselessly from the fountain of life to mingle with the still river of death.

Chapter XXII. A PRINCESS OF LEGEND.

"Is childhood dead?" Lamb asks; "is there not in the best some of the child's heart left, to respond to its earliest enchantments?" Can I now, without a responsive thrill, see myself flash into the unaltered dulness of that Kildare village, a little princess of legend, with the glory of foreign travel about me, the overseas cut of frock and shoes, the haughty and condescending consciousness of superiority?

They were all so visibly at my feet, so glad to worship and admire, so eager to praise, so beset with wonder. I was to spend a week in their midst, a delightful week, as long as a story, as brief as a play, a puff of happiness blown across the bleak wind of solitude, a prolonged and hilarious scamper through sensation as vivid and vital as morning light.

Mary Jane was there, with the unchanged oiled black ringlets, and in my honour she wore them bound with a bright blue ribbon. Louie came out from town to behold me, and gazed in stupefied awe. I had been in a ship across the sea. I had traversed half of England in a railway-carriage. Had I seen an elephant? Mary Jane wanted to know if I had seen the Queen.

No; but I had seen a naked lady, with beautiful golden hair down her back, ride through the town of Lysterby on a white pony, while twelve lovely pages in silver and gold and satin rode before, and twelve lovely maidens with long velvet cloaks lined with white satin rode behind her. This sounded as grand as a royal procession, and I glided ingeniously over the ignominy of having been to England and not having seen the Queen.

Mary Jane's mamma gave me a bowl of milk and a plate of arrowroot biscuits, and as I devoured them, with what a splendid air I recognised the old and faded views of New York! I scorned my past ignorance, and off-handedly mentioned that "You know, the sea isn't a bit like the pond." And then the search for a brilliant and captivating comparison—arm extended to suggest immensity; heaving wave, rolling ship.

"Isn't she wonderful?" they cried; "and the fine language of her!"

From cottage to cottage, from shop to shop, I wandered, intoxicated by the incense of admiration. I embroidered fact and invented fiction with the readiness of the fanciful traveller. Sister

Esmeralda became an unimaginable fiend, who had persecuted me as if I had been the heroine of the fairy-tale I was acting, till the entire village was fit to rise and shout for her blood.

"The likes of that did you ever hear?" a gaunt peasant in corduroy would ask his neighbour in dismay.

"Troth and 'tis thim English as is a quare lot. Beat a little lady as is fit to rule the lot of them, and lock her up in dungeons along with spirits and goblins, and starve the life and soul out of her! Sure 'tis worse they are than in the days of Cromwell."

Naturally, in the amazing record of my experiences, the hidden bones and marble hand of my old friend, the White Lady of the Ivies, played a prominent and shuddering part.

Under the influence of such an audience I tasted the fascinating results of suffering. I was in that brief week repaid for all the previous slights of fortune. I reposed in the lap of adulation, and turned my woes into a dramatic enjoyment. I had suffered; but the romantic activity of my imagination, with a natural mirthfulness of temperament, preserved me from the self-centred and subjective misery of the visionary, and from the embittering anguish of rancour. Once I had excited the local mind against Sister Esmeralda and the wretched superioress of the ladies of Mercy, my anger against them vanished, and they simply remained in memory as picturesque instruments of misfortune. But for the moment I was too full of the joy of living for anything like morbid self-pity. I preferred to loll on the grass beside Bessy the applewoman, and treat all the children of the green to her darling trays of apples with uncle Lionel's bright crown-piece. Bessy never tired of assuring me that I was a wonderful creature, which I fully believed, and Louie made frequent mention of his thirst to be old enough to marry me. It soothed him to hear that he was much nicer than Frank, the horrid Lysterby boy. Louie had not made his first confession, and he was thrillingly and fearfully interested in the tale of mine.

"You know," I dolefully remarked, "the priest won't let you confess any of the nice interesting-looking sins, with the lovely big names, like a-dul-tery and for-ni-fi-ca-tion and de-fraud-ing. He makes you tell awful little sins, like talking in class and answering a nun, and all that sort of thing."

"Oh, but I say," shouted Louie, wagging a remonstrative head, "the priest can't prevent you from saying you committed adultery."

"Yes, but he says you didn't; and then it seems you're telling a lie to the Holy Ghost, and you may be struck dead in the confessional-box."

This Louie regarded as an excessive risk to run for the simple pleasure of confessing a nice big sin. He thought the matter over in bed that night, and communicated to me next morning his intention to confess to having stolen two marbles from Johnnie Magrath, and having licked Tim Martin.

"You know, Angy, I really did lick him, he's such an awful beast, and made his nose bleed rivers, with a black dab under his eyes as big as my fist; and here are the two marbles I stole."

He went back to town that afternoon, with his little gray eyes moist over the brimming smiles of his lively comic mouth. His was a hilarious depression, a rowdy melancholy, emblematic of the destiny in store for him. He grimaced wonderfully, with screwed-up eyelids and twisted and bunched-out lips, and kept on muttering all the time we walked together to the coach-house where the mail-car started from: "It's an awful shame, so it is. A fellow can't do what he likes, but there's always somebody bothering him and ordering him about."

Dear, honest, little playmate! That was the last, last glimpse I had of him. We exchanged our last kiss at the top of the village street, and I wildly waved my handkerchief until a deep bend of the long white Kildare road hid the car, as it seemed to roll off the flat landscape.

Chapter XXIII. MY FIRST TASTE OF FREEDOM.

My parents had taken a house at Dalkey, with a garden a dream of delights, that ran by shadowy slopes and bosky alleys down to the grey rocks where the sea seemed to become our very own, as it rolled over the rocks, and made, from time to time, when the tide ran high, little pools along the sanded fringes of the garden. The house was large and rambling, and of a night when the waves roared and the artillery of the heavens shook at the foundations of earth, it afforded us enormous gratifications of every kind. We were fascinated by terror, and shuddered in silence during the long nights when our parents were kept in town by a theatre, a race, a party. Then we were left in the charge of our eldest sister, a young person of a sentimental and despotic turn of mind. She ruled us with a rod of iron, then invited us to weep with her over the poems of Adelaide Ann Procter. And while she read to us in a tremor of eager sensibilities the legend of Provence, she ruthlessly confiscated "Waverley," "Kenilworth," "Rob Roy," which I kept under my pillow, and read aloud at night to my younger sisters. Novels she held to be the kernel of every iniquity under the sun, but Longfellow and Adelaide Ann Procter were the sole ennobling influences of life. She was sustained in this crooked conviction by a pensive little stitcher, who used to come and sew and mend for us all several hours a-week, and could recite in their entirety "Evangeline" and the "Golden Legend."

A quaint and original figure this white-haired, sad-eyed little stitcher. She had had her romance, stranger than Evangeline's. Her lover had gone to America, and had fought in the Federal war. With a few savings, she followed him across the Atlantic, and sought him out in State after State, walking several leagues a-day, with lifts here and there in waggons, subsisting for months on a daily crust and a root or two, to end her dolorous peregrinations in a hospital with her dying lover's head upon her faithful breast. She returned to Ireland the heroine of a real novel, with black hair bleached and eyes dim from weeping. She had won the right to be cheerless, and stand with flowing eyes "on the bridge at midnight," and tell us "in mournful numbers life is but an empty dream."

We were a wild lot, no doubt, and worked wonders in villainy and mischief. Even our sister's sentimentality at times succumbed to our monstrous spirits; and she forgot Longfellow and Miss Procter, to drop into Irish farce. All the houses round about us were filled with boys and girls of all ages up to sixteen. We needed no introduction to form a general family of some thirty or forty vagrants and imps of both sexes.

The head of the troop was a red-headed youth, destined to adorn the medical profession, and a pale proud-looking boy of fourteen, my first love, Arthur by name, of an exalted family, and now, I believe, a distinguished colonel. When we joined the boys on the cricket-field, I always picked up his balls and handed them to him reverentially, and my reward was to be told in an offhand way that "I was a nice little thing." To me he was Quentin Durward, Waverley, with a dash of Leicester and Prince Ferdinand. He certainly was quite as haughty-looking and distinguished as any of these decorative heroes. His father, an amiable, high-mannered old lord, sometimes treated us to fireworks; and then his sisters, prouder than ever Cinderella's could have been, would come out and smile down benevolently upon us all, with the air of court-ladies distributing prizes at a village festival. Arthur himself was a very simple boy, extremely flattered by my mute adoration, which he encouraged by all sorts of little airs and manœuvres.

It was the red-headed leader who invented the most delightful entertainment in the world. He formed us into a band of beggars. He played a banjo and sang nigger songs, and Arthur, in shirt-sleeves, with a rakish cap rowdily posed on his aristocratic flaxen head, went round with a hat to gather coin. We went from house to house, an excited troop of young rascals, sang and danced and begged and shouted in each garden until the grown-up people appeared and flung a sixpence, sometimes even a shilling, into Arthur's hat. The old lord occasionally rose to half-a-crown. The parents enjoyed the fun as much as we did, and never pretended to recognise us.

What tales we invented! What lies we told! One pretty little girl, with brown ringlets round the rosiest of faces, won a half-sovereign from my stepfather, who was smoking on the lawn when the band invaded his solitude, by assuring his honour that she was "the mother of fourteen children, with their bed-clothes on her back." When she flung the sparkling piece into Arthur's hat, he shouted "Gold!" and a frantic cheer went up from the band. We rushed off in a joyous body next day to Killiney Hill, and had a feast of lemonade and oranges, and toffee and cake. The red-haired chief paid the bill with a flourish, and if there was any change he kept it.

Each parent took his turn in providing the company with an official feast. The old lord monopolised the fireworks. My stepfather instituted races. A wealthy barrister, our neighbour, inveigled a circus for our delectation; and seven delightful old maids, who lived in a kind of castle of their own, outdid all the fathers royally by a regatta of our own. All the boatmen of Dalkey were hired, and each boat ran up a sail. Mighty powers! what a day that was. Were ever youngsters so gratified, so excited, so conscious of being a little community apart, with the sea and the land for its entertainment?

And there was an amiable old judge, who offered us the freedom of his big orchard, where the apples grew in quantities, and we climbed the trees like squirrels, and devoured fruit without fear or restraint.

rode past the door with a crimson cravat, which he fondly hoped to be becoming, and the moody intensity of expression that betokens a broken heart. She minded him not. She was reading "Fabiola" for the hundredth time in the front garden. The gate was open. In his amorous distraction the youth forgot the proprieties, and rode through the gate in lordly style. The door likewise was open, and the pony gallantly galloped into the hall.

My sister's dismay was nothing to the youth's. He stammered and stuttered and went so red that the wonder was he ever grew pale again. But we were used to these commotions aroused by our young Saint Agnes in the bosom of excitable youth. It did not hurt her, and it did not harm them. With gracious gravity she escorted the poor lad to the gate; but we who knew her knew that she was stifling with suppressed laughter. For my eldest sister had a pretty humour, even an irony of her own, and gaiety, as will be seen, was not contraband in her religion.

She constituted herself our veritable mother in that old rambling house of Dalkey. She ruled us like an autocrat, and punished us with a lamentable severity. To teach us self-control and fearlessness, she insisted that the smallest baby should be taken in her night-dress, half asleep, and flung into the wild Irish sea that roared at the foot of the garden. No mercy was shown a recalcitrant babe. Howl she never so dolorously, she was plunged in head-foremost, sputtering salt through her rebellious lips.

At night, when our parents stayed in town, she gathered us together in the long low drawing-room, and insisted that we should examine our consciences, meditate, and say the Rosary aloud to keep away robbers and ghosts. All the boys got to know of this edifying practice, and outside the window a crowd of arch-villains would gather, and shout the responses derisively. We could hear Arthur's high-bred tones sing out "Holy Mary, Mother of God," above the deep bass notes of the red-headed chief. Arthur's brother, an elegant guardsman, staying with the old lord for a couple of weeks, often condescended to join the band of reprobates; and once I peeped out through the big chinks of the shutter, and saw the man of fashion, with the hall-light directly upon his lean and bronzed visage, eyes devoutly lifted to heaven in mimicry of my eldest sister's ecstatic gaze, and hands folded like those of a stained-glass picture: "Holy Mary! pray for me, a miserable sinner. Blessed St. Agnes, help, oh help to convert me!"

Even the devotion of my eldest sister was unsettled, and we could see her mobile lips twitch. It sufficed to reveal to us that the autocrat was off guard, and we lay about the floor, and shrieked with delight.

Whenever he met my eldest sister upon the roads or rocks, the elegant guardsman raised his hat with the air of a prince, and never a hint about him of nocturnal iniquities.

But austere as she was in all things pertaining to discipline and religion, she allowed us unbounded freedom out-of-doors. Some notion of our use of that liberty may be seized from the following ejaculations of an elderly bachelor, a political friend, who came to visit my stepfather, and was confronted with this young saint of the golden locks, the established mistress of a large household.

The elderly gentleman, looking out of the window in front, perceived two little boots dangling from the branch of a high tree, almost against the heaven.

"Who's up that tall tree?" asked the elderly gentleman.

"Oh, that's Angela. She always reads up there."

"Bless my soul!" exclaimed the elderly gentleman.

After further conversation, he walked down the room to examine the view from the back. In gazing across the sea, seemingly near Howth, he detected a rock point surrounded with heavy waves, and two little specks upon this rock.

"It looks as if there were some creatures in danger of being drowned," remarked the elderly gentleman.

"Oh, not at all. That's Pauline's rock. She and Birdie always go out when the tide is out, and spend the whole day wading there, and they come back when the tide runs out again."

"My God!" cried the elderly gentleman.

Looking later up to the stable roof, he saw three little golden heads bent over cards.

"What's that?" he blankly asked.

"Those are the three youngest, playing beggar-my-neighbour on the roof."

"What extraordinary children!" muttered the elderly gentleman.

She devised a notable and original punishment for me

whenever I flew into one of my diabolical rages. She would order Miss Kitty, the sentimental little stitcher, to hold my feet, a servant to hold my head, and while I lay thus on the ground in durance vile, she would piously besprinkle me with holy water, and audibly beseech the Lord and my guardian angel to deliver me of the devil. It would be difficult for me to conceive an operation more suitable as entertainment of the devil than my sister's pious and fiendish method of obtaining his dismissal. The first thing I inevitably did, when liberated, was to go into the yard, and pump all the holy water off my wicked person. Then, dripping like a Newfoundland, I would return to the house and decline to change my dress or shoes, in the vociferated hope of immediate death from consumption.

Chapter XXV. OUR BALL.

All the children and young folk round about us had parents who, if they went into town of a morning, were safe to return at night. Most of them had mothers and aunts who lived at Dalkey all the summer. Only we were happy enough to be so neglected by indifferent parents as to possess a large house at our exclusive disposition four or five entire days and nights of the week. Picture our rare and wild abuse of that freedom, and imagine the envy it inspired in the bosoms of other children, of natures as independent as ours!

"I say," proposed the red-headed chief, "what a capital idea if we had a ball in your house some evening when they're away."

Between my eldest sister and me were two little maids, less of the rascal and less of the saint than either of us. Pauline, the teller of wonderful tales at Lysterby, seized upon the notion with avidity. A ball! our own ball, given by ourselves, and all the vagrant band between the dances refreshed by our ingenious efforts and exploits! It was a grand idea. How we clapped our hands, danced, and stamped our feet in the exuberance of content.

At first Saint Agnes demurred. She, after all, was the head of the house by deputy. Not only was she responsible for our immortal souls, but for our fragile bodies; above all, was she responsible for the state of the larder. It was she who told the servant what to order at the general grocer; she who drew attention to the condition of the cellar, in provision for the horde of Sunday visitors, and the interminable file of eager friends who made a point of inquiring after the health of my parents and their progeny on band nights.

You never understand how extremely popular you are until you are in a position to entertain at a pleasant seaside resort, within easy distance of the metropolis, where a fashionable gathering meets twice a-week to listen to the evening band, and where there are regattas. The most distant acquaintance suddenly remembers that he is your dearest friend. Troops invade your garden; your drawing-room is never empty. Shoals devour the refreshments of your dining-room. At ten o'clock, when you are on the point of barricading your too hospitable doors, men arrive cheerily to bid you the time of day, and claim a whisky-and-soda. I speak of Dublin, naturally, where, as a rule, we begin our afternoon calls at midnight, and where the early awakened lark is safe to find us snoring. Inhabit that same seaside place in winter, and even your dearest friend will forget to remember that he knows you. Irish hospitality is justly famous. There is nothing to match it on the face of the earth. But Irish abuse of hospitality is, perhaps, insufficiently recorded, and there is nothing more speedily forgotten than the unlimited favours of "open house."

My parents kept "open house" with a vengeance, which is the reason to-day that none of us possess the needful sixpence to jingle on the traditional tombstone. It was the reason also that, when our ball came off, we children were in a position to offer our thirty or forty miniature guests flowing bowls of innocuous lemonade by the dozens, ham-sandwiches, boxes of Huntley & Palmer's biscuits, baskets of apples purchased by the hundred by my stepfather from his friend the judge, whose orchards we daily pillaged. There was also claret and soda-water, and even genial port and sherry, for that portion of the community we regarded as "the grown-up,"—Arthur, the red-headed boy, Saint Agnes, Pauline, and a few others of both sexes.

We discovered that my parents designed to sit out a play on a certain evening, which meant that they would never give themselves the trouble to catch the last train, and would sleep in town. Invitations were instantly despatched, Saint Agnes giving her consent reluctantly, but young enough to enjoy the prospect of the escapade. The ball was to open as soon as possible after the seven o'clock tea, for at Dalkey, in those days, all the children dined at two o'clock and sat down at seven to a meal of tea and bread-and-butter, with barmbrack and buttered toast on high holidays.

By eight o'clock the long drawing-room was full. We lit the clusters of tapers round the walls, which were reserved for the pleasures of our elders. The gas flared in every jet of the big chandelier. You might have fancied we were celebrating a Royal birthday, such was the brilliancy of our illuminated ball-room. Arthur had brought down, before tea, bunches of flowers from his father's hothouse, and Saint Agnes was ever a veritable witch in the arrangement of flowers.

The red-haired chief, as master of the ceremonies, wore a huge peony in his buttonhole, and with what gusto he marshalled us about, told off couples, and shouted "Lancers now," or "Look out now, the Caledonian Quadrille." Three quaint little girls had been allowed to come with their governess, who entered heartily into the spirit of the thing, and never left the piano. Quadrille after polka, waltz after schottische, "Sir Roger de Coverley," mazurka, and gallop. And, between the dances, what riotous fun, when we cast ourselves upon the refreshments, and noisy boys risked death and assassination as they opened lemonade and soda-water bottles with a splendid flourish! Our elders might drink themselves to frenzy on whisky and yet remain more sober than we were as we capered and laughed and quaffed big draughts of harmless fluid. And the sandwiches we ate, the biscuits and apples we devoured, the bread-and-butter we munched, and flick, flack! there was Miss Montgomery at the piano, and dozens of little feet were again twinkling about the floor.

I, proud being, danced twice with Arthur. We floundered in amazing fashion through a set of Lancers, the master of ceremonies shouting the while indignantly at our heels. And later he invited me to go through some mysterious measure he called a gallop, which consisted in a wild charge for the other end of the room, helter-skelter, couples knocking each other down delightedly, rolling over each other, and picking one another up in the best of tempers.

And then, as we mopped our faces, and drank lemonade, somebody proposed that I should give an imitation of Mr. Parker. Arthur and I were the only travelled personages of the assembly. He had been to Eton and I had been to Lysterby, and it was his slightly sarcastic voice that determined me. "Oh, I say, by all means. I hear he was a capital fellow that dancing-master of yours, and you do him to a T."

To prove that I did, I began the *chassé-croisé*, to the tune of an imaginary violin, chanting Nora Creina, amid shrieks of approbation. How often since have my friends lamented my missed vocation! On the stage, whether actress or dancer, my fortune would long ago have been made, and as an acrobat I should have won glory in my teens. But old-fashioned parents never think of these things. If you are a girl, and fortune forsakes the domestic hearth, they tell you to go and be a governess, and bless your stars that, thanks to their good sense, you are enabled to earn a miserable crust in the path of respectability. When they find a child with extraordinary mimic capacities, an abnormal physical suppleness, and a passion for the ballet, it does not occur to them that it would be wiser and more humane to seek to turn these advantages to some account, instead of condemning the little wretch to future misery and self-effacement as a governess.

Pauline, who knew every moment of the famous Mr. Parker by heart, wandered out into the front garden with a lad of her own age to look at the stars and talk of their ideal. It was a few minutes after the hourly train from Dublin stopped at Dalkey, and as they sat on the wall discussing their favourite book of the hour, Manzoni's "Betrothed," they saw a large and lofty figure steadily approach the gate. Good heavens! It was my mother. Pauline was a creature of resource, and she had some understanding of that formidable person.

"Quick, quick, Eddie," she whispered. "Run in and tell Agnes to get them all out by the pantry window, which shows into the laneway. I'll keep mamma outside talking about the stars."

Effectively, when my mother opened the gate, she encountered the solemn sentimental regard of a student of the stars. Nothing enchanted my mother more than an unexpected revelation of intelligence in one of her children. She was a woman of colossal intelligence, of wide knowledge, a brilliant talker, and at all times, whatever her temper, you could put her instantly into good-humour, and wean her thoughts from the irritating themes of daily life, by addressing yourself to her intellect, and speaking of remote subjects like the constellations, South Africa, the Federal war, Belgian farming, or the German Empire. She knew everything, was interested in everything, had read everything, could talk like a specialist on any given subject, except mathematics and metaphysics, which she professed to hold in contempt. Another mother would have been staggered to find a girl of thirteen alone beneath the new-lit stars; but my mother found nothing at all odd in being begged to deliver a lecture on astronomy at that hour, and fell into the trap with ingenuous fervour.

And now I beseech you to conceive the scene inside. Ten minutes to clear the house of some thirty excited children, obliged to make a precipitous exit through a narrow pantry window, stifling with hysterical laughter, and in danger of breaking their limbs upon the hard ground as they dropped into the lane that ran alongside the garden into the highroad. Ten minutes to clear the drawing-room of empty bottles and glasses and plates, and put the chairs and tables and couches into order. Ten minutes for us to scamper up-stairs, and get into our night-gear in the dark. Good Lord! what fun! One would willingly endure again the thrashing for those ten brave minutes of fire and fury.

"It was grand!" said Arthur next day to Pauline, after he had tried in vain to look woe-begone over our castigation.

Only the body of the red-headed chief rebelled against the limited space of the pantry window. What puffing and blowing and pushing to get his fat carcass through! "Steady!" shouted the servant, Bridget, a big-boned country girl; and with a bound she ran head-foremost like a charging bull, who meditates the destruction of his enemy. A crash outside, and we thrust anxious heads out of the window to ascertain if the unfortunate youth lay in pieces upon the ground. But no; with smothered laughter he was tearing down the lane for dear life.

With the last evidences of our feast effaced from view, we little ones trod on each other's heels in our flight up-stairs, and staid Agnes went outside, by the way, to induce her mooning sister to go to bed. She simulated the necessary surprise and delight on beholding my mother, and after a few more words upon the heavenly spheres, the three entered the house, now cast, as Agnes fondly believed, into complete darkness.

My mother carelessly explaining why she had decided at the last minute not to sleep in town, turned the handle of the drawing-room door. The tapers, forgotten in the fray, blazed away in all their fatal admission, though the gas of the chandelier had been duly extinguished. The result was that soon the heavenly spheres were round about us instead of on high. Agnes and Pauline rapidly were made to see stars elsewhere than in the sky. When they lay prone and prostrate, not sure that their members were whole, up offended majesty came to us, shivering in our night-dresses. What did it all mean? she wanted to know. Empty bottles heaped up in the pantry corner, a ham vanished, tin boxes empty of their layers of biscuits, knives, plates, glasses, in tell-tale disarray, a broken pane in the pantry window.

We had had our fun, and now came the bad quarter of the hour, when we were expected to pay the bill in beaten flesh. How our ears tingled, our cheeks pained, our heads ached, and our arms smarted! You see it was a very long account, and it took a good deal of blows to make it up. But even the most infuriated creditor is appeased in the long-run, when the gathering in of his dues implies the excessive expenditure of nerve and muscle as such a scene as that of our castigation. The strongest woman cannot beat a half-dozen of children throughout an entire night, and my mother retired, pleased to regard her life in danger by a consequent fit of nervous exhaustion and blood to the head.

Chapter XXVI. THE SHADOWS.

All this hilarity does not imply the total absence of sadness in those bright days. I had lived and suffered too long in solitude not to have reserved a private corner for unuttered griefs, into which no regard of sister or stranger could ever penetrate. It is extraordinary the art with which a circle of children can make one chosen by mutual consent feel in all things, at every moment of the day, an intruder. The two elder than I were sworn friends, the three younger likewise; both groups united as allies. I stood between them, an outsider. I shared their games, it is true, as I shared their meals; but when they had any secrets to impart, I was left out in the cold. I daresay now, on looking back, that had my sullen pride permitted a frank and genial effort, I might easily enough have broken down this barrier. But I was morbidly sensitive, and these young barbarians were very rough and hard. Not ill-natured, but most untender.

I wonder if any other child has been so ruthlessly stabbed by home glances as I. The tale of the Ugly Duckling is, I believe, as common as all the essential legends of human grief and human joy. My dislike of large families is born of the conviction that every large family holds a victim. Amid so many, there is always one isolated creature who weeps in frozen secrecy, while the others shout with laughter. The unshared gaiety of the group is a fresh provocation of repulsion on both sides, and not all the good-will of maturity can serve to bridge that first sharp division of infancy. The heart that has been broken with pain in childhood is never sound again, whatever the sequel the years may offer. To escape the blighting influence of cynicism and harshness is as much as one may hope for; but the muffled apprehension of ache, the rooted mistrust bred by early injustice, can never be effaced.

I cannot now remember the cause of all those dreadful hours, of all those bitter, bitter tears, nor do I desire to recall them. But I still see myself many and many a day creeping under the bed that none might see me cry, and there sobbing as if the veins of my throat should burst. Always, I have no doubt, for some foolish or inadequate cause: a hostile look in response to some spontaneous offer of affection, a disagreeable word when a tender one trembled on my lips, some fresh proof of my isolation, a rough gesture that thrust me out of the home circle as an intruder, and a scornful laugh in front of me as the merry band wandered off among the rocks and left me forlorn in the garden. A robuster and less sensitive nature would have laughed down all these small troubles, and have scampered into their midst imperious and importunate. A healthier child, with sensibilities less on the edge of the skin, not cursed with what the French call an *ombrageux* temper, would have broken through this unconscious hostility, and have captured her place on the domestic hearth—would probably not have been aware of an unfriendly atmosphere.

But this same morbid sensitiveness, mark of my unblessed race, has been the unsleeping element of martyrdom in my whole existence. "Meet the world with a smile," said a wise and genial friend of mine, "and it will give you back a smile." But how can one smile with every nerve torn in the dumb anguish of anticipated pain and slight? How can one smile burdened by the edged sensibilities and nervousness of sex and race, inwardly distraught and forced to face the world, unsupported by fortune, family, or friends, with a brave front? It is already much not to cry. But I shed all my tears in childhood, and left my sadness behind me. When the bigger troubles and tragedies came, as they speedily did, I found sustainment and wisdom in arming myself with courage and gaiety, and so I faced the road. I had then, as ever since, plenty of pleasure to temper unhappiness, plenty of bright rays to guide me through the obscurities of sentiment and suffering. An unfailing beam of humour then and now shed its smile athwart the dim bleak forest of emotions through which destiny bade me cut my way.

One dark moment of peculiar bitterness now makes me smile. I record it as proof of the tiny mole-hills of childhood that constitute mountains. It shows the kind of booby I was, and have ever been, but none the less instructs upon the nature of infant miseries.

We were walking along the road one afternoon with Miss Kitty. A public vehicle tore down the hill led by four horses, three white and one brown. We were four: I the eldest, and my three pretty step-sisters. Birdie shouted—

"Oh, look at the three lovely white horses! That's us three. Angela is the brown horse."

I regarded this choice as a manifest injustice. There was no reason on earth that I should be a brown horse any more than one of my step-sisters. I was angry and sore at what I deemed a slight, and cried—

"I won't be the brown horse. I'll be one of the white horses, or else I'll go away and leave you."

"No, you won't, and you may go if you like. We don't want you. We're three nice white horses."

Here was an instance when I might have laughed down the exclusiveness of these proud babies. But no. I must turn back, and walk home alone, sulky and miserable, nursing my usual feeling of being alone in a cold universe.

An hour of terrible fright for all of us was the morning Birdie fell into Colamore Harbour. We were coming down from Killiney Hill, a lovely spot more prosperous lands might envy us. Birdie walked inside, in a pretty short frock of pale green alpaca, and a new hat with red poppies among the ribbon. In those days Birdie and I ran it closely as infant beauties. Her hair was a shade more flaxen than mine, and the roses of her cheeks a shade paler. She was fatter, too, and less vapoury; but I carried the palm as an ethereal doll, with a classic profile. Alas! the promise of that period was never fulfilled. Both profile and pride of beauty vanished on the threshold of girlhood, to make way for the appearance of a dairymaid in their distinguished stead.

The wall of Colamore Harbour was protected by an iron chain that swung low from the big stones that divided the festoons. Birdie's foot slipped, and the child in a twinkling tumbled over, and plunged, with a hollow crash, into the heavy grey sea. Happily there were bathing-women and fishermen within hail, and as quickly as she had taken an unexpected bath, Birdie was once more in our midst, dripping like a Newfoundland, white and shaking with terror. One of the big boys took her up in his arms and tenderly carried her home. We all followed, awed and hysterical.

My mother was standing in the front garden talking to the gardener, when the party marched in upon her. She frowned as Birdie was deposited on the gravel path in a woeful state—her wet green skirt clinging to her little legs, the discoloured poppies of her hat flat upon the wet ribbon.

"Change that child's clothes," said my mother, indifferently, as if she were all her life accustomed to the sight of a terrified child rescued from the deep, and went on talking to the gardener.

It would be a bold and inhuman assertion to make, and

certainly one I am far from maintaining, that harsh treatment is the proper training of children. But my mother's method has undoubtedly answered better than that of many a tender or self-sacrificing mother. It built us in an admirable fashion for adversity,—taught us to rely upon ourselves, taught us, above all, that necessary lesson, how to suffer and not whine. It is only when I observe how feebly and shabbily a spoiled woman can face trouble and pain, that I feel one may with reason cherish some pride of the power of enduring both with a smile. And when, stupefied and shamed, I contemplate the petty trickeries to which worldliness and untruthfulness can reduce a woman, the infamous devices a slender purse can drag educated ladies into, thus am I partially consoled for the sufferings of childhood. It is much, when one fronts battle, to have been reared in an atmosphere of absolute rectitude, of truthful and honourable instinct. It is a blessing indeed when love includes all this. But bleak as the start was, I would not have had it otherwise at the cost of these great and virile virtues. And since it would appear that the Irish habit of boasting is an incorrigible weakness, and that even in these democratic days my people still persist in descending from kings who have slept in peace over seven hundred years, and may without any extravagant scorn of fact be presumed to have passed for ever into the state of legend, I am glad to acknowledge the priceless debt of common-sense to a Scottish mother. Kings are all very well in their way, especially if they happen to be reigning; but when one learns as authentic fact that an Irish journalist has offered an article to an unknown editor, accompanied with a letter stating that the blood of seven kings runs in his veins, one feels that such a race is all the more rational for a little foreign blood to modify the imperishable and universal blight of royalty.

Chapter XXVII. A DISMAL END OF HOLIDAYS.

For the joy of our small kingdom a delightful Fenian dropped into our midst. It was breathed among us in fatal undertones that he had actually shot a man. He was a figure of romance, if ever there was one. He went about with long boots, and an opera-glass slung over his shoulder. He had lovely dark-blue eyes, which Pauline described as Byronic, and lisped most captivatingly. He was a kind of adopted relative, and, as a special correspondent, has passed into history. He became our elder brother, and in the years to come solaced himself in camp by regarding Agnes as a lost early love. We lay about him on the grass as he told us the tales of the Wonderful Nights. Better still, he invented adventures of his own almost as alarming and enthralling. He told us that he had been to Persia, which was not true—but no matter. We believed in the Persian princess who had swung herself, at the risk of life, from the harem window to become a Christian and marry him; and the king, her royal father, who followed the lovers on horseback and was stabbed in the breast by Edmond's trusty sword. The incoherence of his reminiscences constituted their conspicuous charm. To-day we left him at Samarcand, and on the morrow found him with a fresh and more perilous love-adventure at Constantinople.

It was entrancing.

And then he would offer us a taste of adventure for ourselves: in the absence of our parents he would crowd us into the waggonette, and drive my stepfather's pet horses at a diabolical rate up by the exquisite coast-road of Sorrento, into Bray and through the Wicklow mountains, each curve and hollow and hilly bank menacing to lay us in pieces upon the landscape, and we shouting and hurrahing, in a fond notion that we were offering to the universe the spectacle of the instability of the United Kingdom. Edmond's formidable method of conspiring against the Government at that time consisted in delighting and amusing a troop of little girls!

Foolish, reckless creature, alcohol absorbed and tarnished his brilliant gifts, and his bones lie scattered at far-off Khartoum. He made of a life that might have been a heroic poem a mere trivial legend, and, with his lust for adventure and peril, he met the death he wished for, brief and glorious.

His fear of my mother filled us with a rapturous sense of comradeship, though this fear was quite foolish, for my mother never concealed her preference for his sex, and to men was always as amiable as she was the reverse to us. He beamed and joked with her, but was careful to scan her visage, on the look-out for the first symptoms of storm. The bolt fell rudely upon his shoulders the day he lamed the horses, and did some damage to the waggonette. I never knew what she said to him; but it must have been exceedingly bitter and unbearable, for his cheeks were as white as paper, and his eyes as black as sloes. He was penniless for the moment, and down on his luck, which makes a man more nervously sensitive to slight than in his happier hours.

My stepfather was sorry for him; but, remembering the horses, was relieved to send him off to Spain with a new outfit and the inevitable opera-glasses.

"I shall never forget the old Dalkey garden," he said to Agnes, on the morning of his departure, quite as sentimentally as if he were talking to a grown-up young person. The rascal was always playing a part for his own imagination, and even a slip of a girl of fourteen was better than nobody to regret after a three weeks' stay in a romantically situated house. It was stronger than him. He could not exist without a fancied love-affair on hand.

In the Carlist War, where he claimed to have saved the colours of Spain, rejected the hand of an Infanta, and lent his last five-pound note to Don Carlos, which that illustrious person forgot to return,—'tis a way, he would say musingly, with princes,—as he started for battle, he pathetically adjured his comrades to cut off a lock of his blue-black hair and send it to Agnes, with the assurance that his last thought was given to her. In the pauses of battle he actually entertained himself by composing an imaginary correspondence with an ardent and amorous Agnes, which he read aloud to his dearest friend, with tears in his voice.

But that, as Mr. Kipling in his earlier manner would say, is quite another story, and has nothing to do with the tale of little Angela.

I had no time to lament this fresh eclipse of romance, for Miss Kitty was busy preparing my things for Lysterby, and two days after Edmond's sentimental farewell and departure, I myself most dolefully had said a bitterer good-bye to the rocks and harbour and hills of Dalkey, and had been transported into the town house, to see Mrs. Clement for the last time, and, along with her, make my farewell visit to Kildare.

It was a grievous hour for poor Nurse Cochrane. Jim, her husband, who was down at Wexford two months ago when I came back from Lysterby, had returned a fortnight earlier with death in his eyes.

When we got down at the post-house, the soft fine rain of Ireland was drizzling over the land. A few steps brought us to the top of the green, with the slit of water along the sky and two wild swans visible through the pearl mist. All the blinds of nurse's windows were drawn down, and I instantly recalled a like picture the day Stevie dropped out of life.

The door was open, and a group of working men, in their Sunday suits, were talking in undertones.

"What has happened?" asked Mrs. Clement, alarmed.

"Troth, ma'am, an' 'tis a bad day for herself," said one.

"A power of ill-luck," said another. "A fine young man struck down like that in the flower of youth."

Mrs. Clement hurried inside, and I followed her in excited silence. In the familiar old parlour, with the china dogs and the green spinet, dear kindly nurse sat back in the black horsehair arm-chair, sobbing and moaning in the frantic way peasants will when grief strikes them, and around her in voluble sympathy women hushed and exclaimed and ejaculated, "Glory be to God!" "But who'd think of it?" "Poor Jim! but 'tis himself was the good poor crathur."

I advanced hesitatingly, abashed and frightened by such an explosion of sorrow—I who always went under a bed to weep lest others should mock me. Not then or since could I ever have given expression to such expansive and boisterous feeling, restrained by a fierce and indomitable pride even at so young an age.

Nurse caught sight of me, and held out both hands. I encircled her neck with my arms, and pressed my cheek against hers, and when her sobs had subsided, she stood up, holding me still in a frenzied clasp.

"Come, darling, and look at him for the last time. Poor Jim! He loved you as if you had been his own, his very own, for sure never a child had he."

She took me into Stevie's room, the best bedroom, and on the bed lay a long rigid form. I hardly recognised the dear friendly Jim of my babyhood, on whose knee I so often sat, in the pallid emaciated visage, with the lank black hair round it, and the moustache and beard as black as pitch against the hollow waxen cheek. The same candles were alight upon the table in daytime, and the air yielded the same heavy odour of flowers as on that other day I had penetrated into this room, and found Stevie in his coffin. I shuddered and clung to nurse's skirt, sick with a nameless repulsion, yet I am thankful now that I found courage, when she asked me to kiss him, not to shrink from that simple duty of gratitude. I allowed her to lift me, and I put my mouth to the frozen forehead, with what a sense of fear and horror I even can recall to-day. I was glad to nestle up against Mrs. Clement on the mail-car and press my lips against her live arm to get the cold contact from them. I felt so miserable, so broken was my faith in life, that the return to Lysterby passed unnoticed. I remember neither the departure, the journey, nor the arrival at school.

The episode of my first vacation closed with that dread picture of a dead man and a white shroud, and in the lugubrious illumination of tapers, and nurse sobbing and keening, with no hope of comfort. After that the troubles of home and school looked poor enough, and for some time the nuns found me a very sober and studious little girl. It was long before even Mr. Parker could raise a smile; and Play Day, when we were permitted to do as we liked all day, found me with no livelier desire than to sit still and pore over the novels of Lady Georgiana Fullerton.

Chapter XXVIII. MY FIRST COMMUNION.

This period of unwonted mildness in a turbulent career was seized by the good ladies of Lysterby as a fitting moment for my first communion. It might be only a temporary lull in a course of perversity which would not occur again, and so I was ordered to study anew the lives of the saints. This was quite enough to turn my eager mind from thoughts of daring deed to dreams of sanctity.

I proposed to model my life on that of each fresh saint; was in turn St. Louis of Gonzague, St. Elizabeth of Hungary, St. Theresa and St. Stanislaus of Koscuetzo,—for the life of me I cannot remember the spelling of that Polish name, but it began with a K and ended with an O, with a mad assortment of consonants and vowels between. St. Elizabeth I found very charming, until the excessive savagery of her confessor, Master Conrad, diminished my enthusiasm. When I came to the barbarous scene where Master Conrad orders the queen to visit him in his monastery, which was against the monachal law, and then proceeds to thrash her bare back while he piously recites the Miserere, I shut the book for ever, and declined upon the spot to become a saint.

Nevertheless I made my first communion in a most edifying spirit. I spent a week in retreat down in the town convent, and walked for hours up and down the high-walled garden discoursing with precocious unctuousness to my good friend Mother Aloysius, who, naïve soul, was lost in wonder and admiration of my gravity and sanctimoniousness. I meditated and examined my conscience with a vengeance. I delighted in the conviction of my past wickedness, and was so thrilled with the sensation of being a converted sinner that, like Polly Evans, gladly would I have revived the medieval custom of public confession. Contrition once more prompted me to pen a conventional letter of penitence, submission, affection, and promise of good behaviour to my mother, which virtuous epistle, like a former one, remained without an answer.

This was part of the extreme sincerity of my mother's character. She wished her children, like herself, to be "all of a piece," and did not encourage temporary or sensational developments in them. Since she never stooped to play for herself or the gallery the part of fond mother, she kept at bay any inclination in us to dip into filial sentimentalism. Never was there a parent less likely to kill the fatted calf on the prodigal's return.

And then, in wreath and veil and white robe, with downcast

eyes and folded hands to resemble the engraving of St. Louis of Gonzague, I walked up the little chapel one morning without breakfast. The harmonium rumbled, the novices sang, the smell of flowers and wax was about me, incense sent its perfumed smoke into the air, and I lay prostrate over my prie-dieu, weeping from ecstasy. I fancied myself on the rim of heaven, held in the air by angels. I have a notion now that I wanted to die, so unbearable was the ache of spiritual joy. I was literally bathed in bliss, and held communion with the seraphs.

It seemed a vulgar and monstrous impertinence to be carried off, after such a moment, to the nuns' refectory and there be fed upon buttered toast and crumpets and cake. With such a feast of good things before me I could not eat. I wanted to go back to the chapel and resume my converse with the heavenly spheres. Instead, Mother Aloysius invited me out to the garden, and there spoke long and earnestly, in her dear, simple, kindly way, of my duties as a Christian. I was no longer a bad troublesome child, but a little woman of eleven, with all sorts of grave responsibilities. I was to become disciplined and studious, check my passion for reading, take to sewing, and cultivate a respectful attitude to my superiors. She owned that for the moment I was a model of all the virtues, but would it last long, she dubiously added.

Wise woman! It did not last long. The normal child is occasionally bad and generally good. I reversed the order, and was only very occasionally good and generally as bad as possible. The period of temporary beatification over, I was speedily at loggerheads again with my old enemy Sister Esmeralda. Would you know the cause of our last and most violent quarrel? Lady Wilhelmina of the Abbey had a little girl of my age, so like me that we might have been twin-sisters. Because of this strange resemblance, Lady Wilhelmina often invited me up to the Abbey to play with her daughter Adelaide. She was a dull, proud child, whom I rather despised, but we got through many an afternoon comfortably enough, playing cricket with her brother Oswald. One Sunday after benediction, Adelaide and I were walking side by side when we came near Sister Esmeralda talking to an elder pupil.

"Isn't it wonderful that those children should be so alike!" exclaimed the girl. "They might be twins."

"Not at all," cried Sister Esmeralda, tartly. "Lady Adelaide is far handsomer than Angela, who is only a common little Irish thing."

The words were not meant for my hearing, but they stung me as a buffet. I flashed back like a wild creature on flame, and stood panting in front of my enemy, while Adelaide, pale and trembling, caught my dress behind.

"I heard what you said, and it's a lie. I'm not a common little Irish thing. I am just as good as Lady Adelaide—or you, or anybody else. The Irish are much nicer than the English any day, ever so much nicer,—there, and I hate you, so I do."

"Oh, Angela!" sobbed Adelaide, clutching at my dress.

"Let me alone, you too!" I screamed, beside myself with passion. "I don't care whether you are handsomer than I, for you're just an ordinary little girl, not half as clever as I."

Adelaide, who had a spirit of her own, retorted in proper fashion, and before Sister Esmeralda had time to shake me and push me in before her, I struck the poor little aristocrat full on her angry scarlet cheek.

I was only conscious of the enormity of my fall on receiving a tender almost broken-hearted note from Mother Aloysius. "Dearest child," it lovingly ran, "what has become of all your good resolutions? What about all those nice sensible promises of gentle and submissive behaviour you made me down here in the garden? Is that how St. Louis of Gonzague, St. Elizabeth of Hungary, would have acted? Tell Sister Esmeralda how sorry you are; and write, like my good little Angela, and tell me you are sorry too."

I penned with great care a fervent and honest reply, which I begged Miss Lawson, the lay teacher, to carry to my friend in town. "I'm sorry, ever so sorry, because you are sorry, and you are the only person here I love. But I won't be sorry for Sister Esmeralda. I hate her. She said I was a common little Irish thing. It's mean and nasty, for I am only a child and can't hurt her, and she's big and can hurt me. If I am Irish, I am as good as her."

Chapter XXIX. THE LAST OF LYSTERBY AND CHILDHOOD.

My mother came over again to Lysterby with Pauline and Birdie, who shared my last year in that quaint old town. My mother's second visit is a vague remembrance. I recall a singular old gentleman who joined us in an expedition to Guy's Cliff, and terrified the life out of us girls by a harrowing description of the hourly peril he walked under, and a fervid assurance that he might drop down dead at that very moment of speech. We walked behind him in frozen fear, and looked each moment to see him drop dead at our feet, but my mother discoursed in front of us quite unconcerned. He wore a cloak with a big cape, and said "Madam" after every second word. Guy's Cliff I remember as a lovely place; but the chill water of the well was not so chill as my blood while I contemplated that doomed old man.

Pauline's latest enthusiasm was Miss Braddon, and what glorious things she made of "Lady Audley's Secret," "Aurora Floyd," and, I fancy, a tale about a Captain Vulture! I read these books afterwards (that is the two first), and what poor tawdry stuff, my faith, compared with the brilliant embroideries of my most imaginative sister, who turned lead into pure gold!

Years, how many, many years, after, a man of European fame, one of the rare figures that go to make up a century's portraits, speaking of Pauline, said she was the cleverest woman he had ever known. But alas! alas! hers was not a cleverness a woman poor and obscure could utilise. A man, she would have been a great statesman, for she was a born politician. Geography was her passion, history her mania,—not that she could ever have written history, for she was too quick, complex, and vital to learn so slow a trade as that of a writer's; but hers was a miraculous intuitive seizure of history, that made it to her imperious vision present, and not the smallest historical fact in Europe escaped her attention and remembrance. Could crowned heads but know what a severe and unflinching gaze was fixed upon them! of what singular and passionate importance to her was the marriage of their most distant relatives! Modern history and modern politics became to her what classical music had been to our daft grandfather, whom she strongly resembled. They absorbed her, filled the long, long days of sick and lonely maidenhood, when, such was the vividness, the surprising vitality of her matchless imagination, that in a dull seaside residence she found, and lived and died in, her own excitements and gratifications of mind and soul.

Miss Lawson before leaving the convent had inoculated us, the little ones, her devoted admirers, with a curious passion for pinafored mites—whist. Whist for several months became the object of our existence. Lessons in comparison were but a trivial occupation. When Birdie and I next went home, we taught the game to still smaller mites, and such were the gamblers we became, that we have played whist, I the eldest of the four confederates, twelve, with renowned and aged clubmen, who found us their match. We slept with a pack of cards under our pillow, and dawn found us four little night-dressed girls gathered together in one bed with the lid of a bandbox over our joined knees, rapturously playing whist.

On the pretext of meeting our father at the station of Dalkey every evening at half-past six, we took possession of the waiting-room, cards in hands, and imperiously acquainted our friend the station-master with the fact that the room was engaged. The novelty of the situation so tickled the station-master that while we four miscreants in short skirts played our game of whist, not a soul was allowed to enter the waiting-room—an injustice I now marvel at.

The boys and girls around us were neglected. We only cared for whist, which we played from the time we got up until we went to bed, with no other variation that I remember except sea-bathing and Captain Marryat's novels. As none of the boys or girls shared our desperate passion, it followed that I and my three smaller step-sisters became inseparable, and held all our fellows who did not live for whist to be poor dull creatures. Once we made part of a children's gathering at Killiney Hill, but after the cold chicken, jelly, cakes, and lemonade, we speedily found life intolerable without a pack of cards.

"I say, Angela," whispered Birdie to me, when I was musing of honours and the odd trick, "I've brought them. Let's go behind a tree and have a game."

Now I always take a hand with pleasure because of that defunct vice; but, alas! I am compelled to own that I never played so well as at eleven.

My next passion, for which Pauline this time was responsible, was genealogy. We invented a family called the L'Estranges and brought them over with the Conqueror. Where they had previously come from we did not ask. What did it matter? To come over with the Conqueror was, we knew, a certificate of chivalry. The chief, Walter, fought at the Battle of Hastings. We pictured him with golden locks, a bright and haughty visage, stern grey eyes that could look ineffably soft in a love-scene, and beautiful shining armour. We married him to a certain Saxon Edith, and down as far as the Battle of Bosworth Field, Walter and Edith were the favourite family names of the L'Estranges. To give piquancy to our most delightful game, and stimulate our imagination, we founded a cemetery of the L'Estranges. We made little wooden tombstones, on which we carved imaginary epitaphs of all the imaginary L'Estranges who had died since the Battle of Hastings. As we loathed old people in our dramatic history, except the aged lord who dies blessing a numerous progeny from time to time, all our resplendent heroes perished in romantic youth on the Spanish Main, on battle-fields, on the African coast; or rescuing Turkish princesses, or capturing Grecian isles; while their brides invariably faded away either of consumption or a broken heart at seventeen. The cemetery was peopled to excess by the time we got as far as the Battle of Bosworth Field, where the last hero fell in front of the enemy before he had time to marry the maiden of his choice.

It is astonishing how little the average child approves of a natural death. The heroes must die by violence in the flower of youth, and the heroines must perish or pine away from unnatural causes on the threshold of maidenhood. Nineteen is even old and commonplace: the age of glory is seventeen.

If you entered our garden, turned into the cemetery of the L'Estranges, you would have seen layer upon layer of little wooden sticks that looked like the indication of hidden seeds, and if you stooped to read the legend, this is the sort of thing that would have greeted your eyes:—

"Here lies Walter l'Estrange" (or Rupert, or Ralph, or Reginald, for we were fond of these names), "born such and such a year, wrecked off the coast of Barbary such and such a year," or "perished in a conflict with Spanish pirates," &c.; and beside him, with day and date of birth and burial, "Here lies Edith, his beloved wife, daughter of Lord Seymour or Admiral So-and-so."

In a big ledger, recorded in Pauline's sprawling calligraphy, were the lives and characters of the imaginary dead. It was remarkable that all our heroes were as brave as lions, as modest and mild as lambs, and as stainless as Galahads. To lend relief to the monotony of their implacable virtue, we now and then invented a villain, who invariably died in a vulgar brawl or a duel. The battlefield, the Spanish Main, the rescue of Turkish princesses, and a noble shipwreck, were kept for the Galahads.

The last profile of my Lysterby days is that of a radiant and lovely Irish girl, who came from Southampton, the Mother House of the Ladies of Mercy, to stay with us until the nuns found her a situation as governess. Her name was Molly O'Connell: she was doubly orphaned almost since birth, her mother having died giving life to her, and her father within the following year. Everybody about her thought it very sad that her mother should have died on the very day of her birth. But I, alas! knew a sadder thing. My father, who, I am told, was a very kindly, tender-hearted man, died some months before my birth. Had I been given the choice beforehand, and known what was in store for me, I should have greatly preferred it had been my mother who died many months before my birth. But, alas! babies in the ante-natal stage are never consulted upon the question of their own interest.

Molly O'Connell remains upon memory as beauty in a flash. Never since have I seen such a flashing combination of brilliant effects. Oh! such teeth—teeth to dream of, teeth that laughed and smiled, that had a sort of light in them like white sunshine, and were the fullest expression I have ever known of the word radiance! Then her eyes were pools of violet light, where you seemed to see straight down to the bottom of a deep well, violet all the way down to the very end, where you saw yourself reflected. These glorious eyes, like the teeth, smiled and laughed; they caressed, too, looked an unfathomable tenderness and sweetness, shone, irradiated like stars, went through the whole gamut of visual emotion, from the holiest feeling, the effable eloquence of sentiment, to the bewildering obscurities of passion. They were eyes, I now know, to damn a saint, and—Heaven help us all in a world so inexplicable as ours!—they performed their fatal mission to the bitter end. Add to these eyes and teeth hair as dark as shadow, as thick as the blackness of night, a scarlet and white face, round and dimpled, of the divinest shape, the rarest and ripest combination of fruit and flower, with deep peach-like bloom upon the soft cheek, and the hue of a crimson cherry upon the curved full lips, and there you have a woman equipped for her own destruction, if she have a heart to lose, no brains to speak of, and only as much knowledge of man, of the world, as a fresh-born kitten or a toddling babe.

Molly was the joy, the light, the glory, the romance of our lives. We worshipped her for her unsurpassable loveliness, which kept rows of young eyes fixed upon her charming visage in round-lidded, wonder and awe; we adored her for her gaiety, her chatter, her incessant laughter, and we loved her for the conviction that she was as young and innocent and helpless and unlettered as ourselves.

Molly was nineteen, but she was a bigger child than any of us; and now I hold my breath in pain when I remember the nature and quality of her innocence. She had been brought up from infancy in a convent. Had her life lain among the roses, such ignorance as hers might be pardoned in her teachers. But to send out into the world, to earn her living among selfish and indifferent strangers, a young girl of such bewildering exquisiteness, and never once hint to her the kind of perils that would beset her, give her no knowledge of man, nor of herself, nor of nature! This is an iniquity the nuns of Southampton can never be pardoned.

Now that I know the sequel, and understand what the beginning meant, I cannot recall our laughter over Molly's first experiences without a thrill of horror. The nuns had placed her with titled folk—Lord and Lady E., with whom lived Lady E.'s father, an old earl, a widower. Molly was the most ingenuous and garrulous of creatures. She spent her first vacation some months later with us, and kept us at recreation hour in shouts of laughter and scorn over her adventures. The old earl was the most extraordinary old man, according to her. He was always meeting her alone, here, there, and everywhere. She seemed to think it was a sort of schoolboy's game. Once he showed her in the garden, when no one was by, a splendid diamond bracelet, which he had bought for her.

"O Molly!" we all screamed in joy, "he wants to marry you, and you'll be a grand countess, like the gipsy maiden of the song."

But Molly curled her lips haughtily. Did we know that he was seventy, a queer old gentleman, just fit to be tucked into bed and given gruel? The suspicion of evil design never once entered her innocent head, for the simple reason that she had not the ghost of a suspicion of any kind of evil.

Then Lady E. went up to town, and left this bewitching creature at the mercy of her husband. Molly again regarded it in the light of a capital game. The aged earl and his middle-aged son-in-law appeared to be on strained terms. The poor goose never suspected why. Lord E. insisted on her sitting in his wife's place at table—and still she suspected nothing.

One night, she told us, shrieking with laughter as at the height of the grotesque, Lord E. mistook her room for the nursery, and entered it in his shirt. Not the faintest feeling of anger or fear on the part of this blind, silly maid. All she did was to go into convulsions of laughter, "because he looked so ugly and so ridiculous." But it was still part of the high old game of life, where everything happens to send one into fits of laughter. That tears, that trouble, that shame and blighting misery lay in wait for her, this radiant, unconscious, ignorant, and foolish innocent could not then suspect.

We, too, thought it a splendid game, laughed heartily at the ridiculous figure she described Lord E. as cutting in his nightshirt, agreed with her that the old earl was a monstrous old fool to go skipping in that absurd way down the park avenues with her, putting his hand upon his heart, sighing and talking in a wild incoherent way about "the loveliest girl on earth," whom Molly, the least vain of creatures, never for one moment suspected was herself. For she was far too busy laughing at people to understand them. You had but to stand solemnly before her, and say, "It's a wet day," and off she was on a ringing cascade. What you said she probably did not understand in the least; but the expression of your eye, the tone of your voice, made her laugh.

And so the infamous nature of the pursuit of the earl and his son-in-law quite escaped her, and neither the diamond bracelet, nor Lord E. in his shirt at night in her room, awoke the faintest throb of alarm. All this to her and us was part of the eternal joke of nature. And a very, very few years afterwards, I learned, one who had loved her well and sought her far discovered her at night in the vicinity of the Haymarket, with paint upon her cheeks and lips, and the fatal brightness of consumption looking out of her hollow violet eyes.

My remembrance of the rest of my stay at Lysterby fades away upon the heavy perfume of incense in the cold aisles of the cathedral, whither we were conducted by the nuns for the breathlessly interesting offices of Holy Week. It is a long dream of sombre tones and solemn notes, which I followed in a passionate absorption in the "Offices of Holy Week," printed in Latin and

English, for which I paid the sum of four shillings. I studied those offices so diligently, followed them so accurately, that afterwards I could detect to a movement, a note, a Latin word, any error or omission in the Lenten services of the pro-cathedral of Dublin, where I must say the rites struck me as shorn of all impressiveness.

But at Lysterby functions were rigidly correct. The evening office of Tenebræ was a funereal delight. The services of Maundy Thursday, Good Friday, and Holy Saturday were religious excitements on which to live for months. I shut my eyes, even now in middle age, and I see again the long grey cathedral aisles dim in taper-light, altars hung in black, and the lean aristocratic visage of Father More above the surplice and violet stole, and I hear him chant in his thin, melodious voice, "Oremus, flectamus genua!" and listen again for the response, "Levate!"

I cannot precisely define my sensations in this period. Religion with me was nothing but an intense emotion nourished upon incense, music, taper-lit gloom, and a mysterious sense of the intangible. It was in the fullest meaning of the word sensuous; but while its attraction lasted, nothing I have since known could be compared with it for intensity. While under its spell, you seem to float in the air, to touch the wings of the angels, to be yourself part of the heavenly sphere you aspire to attain. Rapture itself is a mean enough word to define your emotions. And then you come back to earth with a sense of unspeakable deception and surprise. You feel hungry, and loathe yourself for the vulgar need. Your ear is buffeted by loud earthly sounds instead of the roll of the organ and the monotonous solemnity of Gregorian chant.

To realise this is to understand how so many sentimental, virtuous, and sensuous souls seek oblivion of life in religious excitement. It is a mental and moral mixture of opium and alcohol extremely soothing to the bruised consciousness, a gentle diversion in common-place cares that poor humanity must not be begrudged; though, as George Eliot has finely said, it is proof of strength to live and do well without this narcotic.

The return to Ireland coincides with the outbreak of the Franco-German war. A mist hangs over those terrible months, but Dublin I remember was French to a man. Every morning my eldest sister marched us off to mass to pray for the French, and we wept profusely over each tragic telegram. Our hero Edmond was over there, fighting and lying with equal gallantry. Several noble dames had tended his wounds and offered to marry him, and he escaped from prison with the assistance of the jailer's daughter, who loved him despairingly. I recall our awed inspection of several helmets and swords brought back from the war by a quantity of heroic young Irishmen who professed to have laid the Germans low on countless occasions. I do not now know what they did out there, for there is always a great deal of Tartarin, an atmosphere of Tarascon, about the Irishman returned from abroad. But we all went down in a glorified body, dressed in our very best, to assist at the arrival of Marshal M'Mahon and his wife, who came all the way from far-off France to thank us for what they had or had not done.

Here, at the age of twelve, my childhood ends, and youth, troubled youth, begins.

* * * * * * * *

To stand upon the hill-top and cast a glance of retrospection down the long path travelled in all its excess of light and shadow; impenetrable darkness massed against a luminous haze through which rays of blazing glory filter, each one striking upon memory in a shock of prismatic hues, until the eye reaches as far back as the start from the valley,—how astonished we are at the unevenness of the road! So brilliant, so ineffectual for most of us, is this dear thing called Youth! The uneasy flutter from the nest, the wild throb of pulses, now for ever tamed, at each sharp encounter with fate; the courage, the hope, the passion—alas! how futile and how sad to eyes in middle life that see the inexorable word "failure" written across that splendid tear-blotted page of strife, of yearning, of frailty and endeavour. Seen from the hill-top, how small the big stones are that broke our path! How easy it might have been to skirt the thorn-bushes and brambles, instead of tearing an impulsive way through them, and falling so repeatedly on bleeding face and hands!

Impatience and panting courage have served to carry us through the unequal battle, and now, resting in the equable tones of middle life, how sweet a wonder seem the blackness, the purple, the golden lights of youth! We sit in the unemotional shade, and slake our thirst for the old joys and sorrows by fondly recalling the ghosts of dead hours and dead dreams, of forgotten faiths and dim-remembered faces; and though we may not desire to re-live each year with its burden of pains and pangs, surely we may tell ourselves that it is good to have lived those past years, even if tears seem the most prominent part of our inheritance.

Then, however sad the living moment, we still had the consolation of that beautiful and vision-bearing word "To-morrow." In youth, sorrow fells us to-day, and joy awakes us to-morrow. It is always—Land may be in sight to-morrow! The night is dark, but hope dances blithely through our veins with the delicious assurance that to-morrow brings the sun. The world is empty, but vague dreams tell us that to-morrow love will cross our path and fill the universe. Hope is the magician that waved us forward and carried us recklessly through briar and bramble, with undaunted confidence in life, in ourselves, and in all things around us. Each fall was ever the last, each pang the precursor of eternal happiness.

And now it is over. Hope's magic wand for us is broken, and she has folded her wings and dropped into slumber that wakens not again: henceforth our best friend is drab-robed content.

THE END.

CPSIA information can be obtained
at www.ICGtesting.com
Printed in the USA
LVHW081505161020
669005LV00028B/1307

Chapter XXIV. MY ELDEST SISTER.

My eldest sister was only fourteen, but she was already, had ever been, a sage and a saint. At the age of eight she had put her hand into a blazing fire in order to die the death of a Christian martyr. She shrieked dismally for several hours afterwards. Another time, staying with relatives in the country, she knelt in the gloaming in a big barn, praying with fervently closed eyes, in the hopes of being devoured by lions. She heard the distant growlings of an angry mastiff, and thought her prayer was granted, and that this was the ravening lion about to make a meal of her. She fell down in a fit of convulsions, and had to be nursed by several doctors.

When she came back to consciousness, with her hair shorn and wan little hands upon the coverlet, she recognised our tender mother seated beside her bed, and contentedly shortening her last new frock for my second sister. She offered up the mortification for her sins, and instantly said a prayer to her patron saint, Agnes. At dinner she never ate pudding or pie, not even damson-pie, for which I in those gluttonous days would have sold, not only my own soul, but hers as well; but after dinner she invariably carried her share of these luxurious edibles to the nearest poor person.

She visited the poor continually, always provided with tea and sugar and such things; and Pauline, who accompanied her on these missions of mercy, assured me that she often saw the pet cases of misery dash under the bed excellent dishes of bacon and eggs and bottles of Guinness' stout, while the traditional invalid would jump into bed, gather the clothes about her, and begin to whine, "Sure, your little ladyship, 'tis our lonesome selves as hasn't had bit or sup since last we saw your purty face."

My eldest sister was a bewitching beauty. She had large dusky blue eyes in constant communion with the heavenly spheres. She had ruddy golden hair that shown adown her back like pounded guineas, and her complexion was a thing to gape at. Indeed we had all inherited from our mother wonderful golden locks and dazzling complexions.

This sentimental and saintly creature wrought the utmost havoc around her, and went dreamily through life unconscious or sublimely indifferent, with her gaze of impassioned sadness fixed upon her heavenly home. Youths went down before her like ninepins, and trembled when they addressed her. One lad of sixteen